초등에서

브릿지
BRIDGE VOCA
보카

중등으로

| Advanced |

How to Use 브릿지 보카

① 단어 학습과 Daily Test

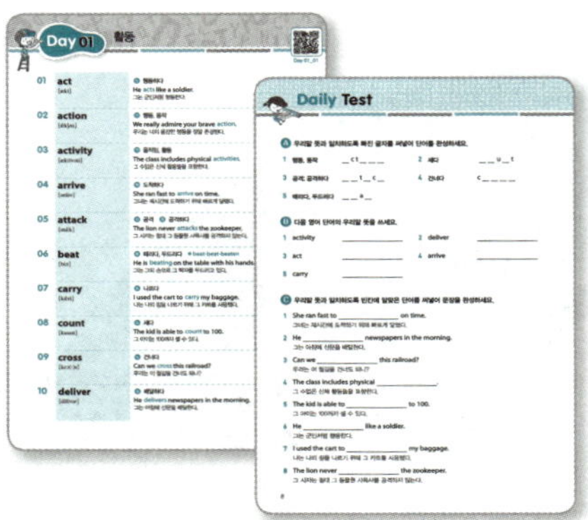

하나의 Day는 20단어로 구성되어 있습니다.
암기 부담을 줄이기 위해 10단어씩 나누어 학습합니다.
원어민의 발음으로 녹음된 단어와 예문을
QR코드를 통해 들으면서 정확한 발음을 익히고,
문장 활용 능력을 키울 수 있습니다.

② Review

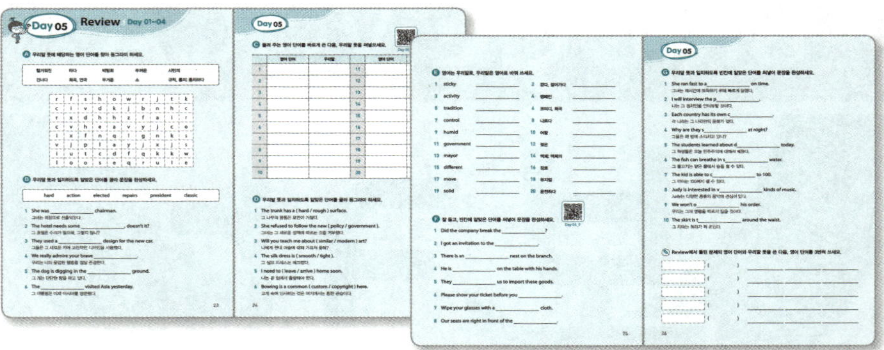

4일 학습 후 5일째에는 지금까지 배운 단어들을 확실하게 복습합니다. Word Search, 문장 완성하기,
받아쓰기 등 다양한 유형의 문제를 풀면서 단어들을 다시 한 번 머릿속에 새깁니다.

③ Index

단어들을 알파벳 순으로 수록하여,
특정 단어를 빠르게 찾을 수 있습니다.

 이 교재의 모든 음원은 메가북스 홈페이지에서
무료 MP3파일로도 다운받을 수 있습니다.

Contents와 학습 진도표

브릿지 보카 시리즈 구성

Day	권 구성	Basic	Intermediate	Advanced
01		사람	음식	활동
02		수업	동물과 식물	사물 묘사
03		취미와 여가	여행과 휴가	문화
04		음식	쇼핑	정치
05		Review	Review	Review
06		가족	장소	자연환경
07		과일과 채소	대인 관계	상황 묘사
08		동물	학교	우주와 과학
09		일상생활	나라와 지역	경제
10		Review	Review	Review
11		식물과 곤충	순서	일의 진행
12		날씨	건물과 건축물	국제 사회
13		음악	가정	상태
14		집	사회생활	생각과 인지
15	주제	Review	Review	Review
16		패션	시장	인물 묘사
17		운동	건강과 질병	위치와 방향
18		얼굴과 인물 묘사	의사소통	달력
19		감정	때와 시기	의견
20		Review	Review	Review
21		감각	크기	교통
22		움직임과 동작	안전과 사고	감정
23		미술	요일과 계절	제작과 판매
24		신체	자연 현상	동네와 길 찾기
25		Review	Review	Review
26		모양과 색깔	성격	행사와 시간
27		숫자	직업	능력
28		생활용품	얼굴과 인물 묘사	대중문화
29		직업	회사	필수 부사
30		Review	Review	Review
31		-ail, -ain	bl-, cl-, fl-, pl-	-ar-
32		-eat, -eed	cr-, dr-, fr-	-er
33	Phonics	-ight, -ind	sk-, sm-, sn-, sp-	-ir-
34		-one, -ore	kn-, -gn, -mb, wr-	-or-, -ur-
35		Review	Review	Review

주제별 Check

Day 01~30

오늘 외운 단어를 내일은 몇 개나 기억할 수 있을까요?
하나의 주제와 연관된 단어들을 모아서
의미를 이해하며 외워 보세요.
단어들이 꼬리에 꼬리를 물고 연상되어
오래 기억할 수 있어요.
24가지 주제에 따라 구분된 480단어를
머릿속에 쏙쏙 넣어 보세요.

하나 더! 철저한 복습으로 잊혀져 가는 단어를
확실하게 내 것으로 만들어요.

 **Day 01** 활동

01 act
[ækt]

동 행동하다
He acts like a soldier.
그는 군인처럼 행동한다.

02 action
[ǽkʃən]

명 행동, 동작
We really admire your brave action.
우리는 너의 용감한 행동을 정말 존경한다.

03 activity
[æktívəti]

명 움직임, 활동
The class includes physical activities.
그 수업은 신체 활동들을 포함한다.

04 arrive
[əráiv]

동 도착하다
She ran fast to arrive on time.
그녀는 제시간에 도착하기 위해 빠르게 달렸다.

05 attack
[ətǽk]

명 공격 동 공격하다
The lion never attacks the zookeeper.
그 사자는 절대 그 동물원 사육사를 공격하지 않는다.

06 beat
[bi:t]

동 때리다, 두드리다 ✿ beat-beat-beaten
He is beating on the table with his hands.
그는 그의 손으로 그 탁자를 두드리고 있다.

07 carry
[kǽri]

동 나르다
I used the cart to carry my baggage.
나는 나의 짐을 나르기 위해 그 카트를 사용했다.

08 count
[kaunt]

동 세다
The kid is able to count to 100.
그 아이는 100까지 셀 수 있다.

09 cross
[krɔ(:)s]

동 건너다
Can we cross this railroad?
우리는 이 철길을 건너도 되니?

10 deliver
[dilívər]

동 배달하다
He delivers newspapers in the morning.
그는 아침에 신문을 배달한다.

Daily Test

A 우리말 뜻과 일치하도록 빠진 글자를 써넣어 단어를 완성하세요.

1 행동, 동작   __ c t __ __ __ __   **2** 세다   __ __ u __ t

3 공격; 공격하다   __ __ t __ c __   **4** 건너다   c __ __ __ __

5 때리다, 두드리다   __ __ a __

B 다음 영어 단어의 우리말 뜻을 쓰세요.

1 activity   _________________   **2** deliver   _________________

3 act   _________________   **4** arrive   _________________

5 carry   _________________

C 우리말 뜻과 일치하도록 빈칸에 알맞은 단어를 써넣어 문장을 완성하세요.

1 She ran fast to _________________ on time.
그녀는 제시간에 도착하기 위해 빠르게 달렸다.

2 He _________________ newspapers in the morning.
그는 아침에 신문을 배달한다.

3 Can we _________________ this railroad?
우리는 이 철길을 건너도 되니?

4 The class includes physical _________________.
그 수업은 신체 활동들을 포함한다.

5 The kid is able to _________________ to 100.
그 아이는 100까지 셀 수 있다.

6 He _________________ like a soldier.
그는 군인처럼 행동한다.

7 I used the cart to _________________ my baggage.
나는 나의 짐을 나르기 위해 그 카트를 사용했다.

8 The lion never _________________ the zookeeper.
그 사자는 절대 그 동물원 사육사를 공격하지 않는다.

11 drive
[draiv]

동 운전하다 ✿ drive-drove-driven
They have to drive safely.
그들은 안전하게 운전해야 한다.

12 enter
[éntər]

동 들어가다, 들어오다
Please show your ticket before you enter.
들어가기 전에 당신의 표를 보여 주세요.

13 follow
[fálou]

동 따라가다, 따라오다
All the kids are following their teacher.
그 모든 아이들은 그들의 선생님을 따라가고 있다.

14 leave
[liːv]

동 떠나다, 출발하다 ✿ leave-left-left
I need to leave home soon.
나는 곧 집에서 출발해야 한다.

15 move
[muːv]

동 움직이다, 옮기다
The ants can't move the stone.
그 개미들은 그 돌멩이를 옮길 수 없다.

16 practice
[prǽktis]

명 연습 동 연습하다
She practiced the harp until midnight.
그녀는 자정까지 하프를 연습했다.

17 repair
[ripέər]

동 수리하다 명 수리
The hotel needs some repairs, doesn't it?
그 호텔은 수리가 필요해, 그렇지 않니?

18 ride
[raid]

동 타다 ✿ ride-rode-ridden
We enjoy riding on the big boat.
우리는 그 큰 배에 타는 것을 즐긴다.

19 shout
[ʃaut]

동 소리치다
Why are they shouting at night?
그들은 왜 밤에 소리치고 있니?

20 walk
[wɔːk]

동 걷다, 걸어가다
Penguins are walking toward the ocean.
펭귄들이 바다 쪽으로 걸어가고 있다.

Daily Test

A 우리말 뜻과 일치하도록 빠진 글자를 써넣어 단어를 완성하세요.

1 움직이다, 옮기다   _ _ v _

2 수리하다; 수리   _ e _ a _ _

3 걷다, 걸어가다   _ _ _ k

4 운전하다   _ r _ v _

5 소리치다   s _ _ _ _

B 다음 영어 단어의 우리말 뜻을 쓰세요.

1 enter   _________________

2 leave   _________________

3 ride   _________________

4 follow   _________________

5 practice   _________________

C 우리말 뜻과 일치하도록 빈칸에 알맞은 단어를 써넣어 문장을 완성하세요.

1 They have to _________________ safely.
그들은 안전하게 운전해야 한다.

2 Penguins are _________________ toward the ocean.
펭귄들이 바다 쪽으로 걸어가고 있다.

3 Please show your ticket before you _________________.
들어가기 전에 당신의 표를 보여 주세요.

4 She _________________ the harp until midnight.
그녀는 자정까지 하프를 연습했다.

5 We enjoy _________________ on the big boat.
우리는 그 큰 배에 타는 것을 즐긴다.

6 All the kids are _________________ their teacher.
그 모든 아이들은 그들의 선생님을 따라가고 있다.

7 Why are they _________________ at night?
그들은 왜 밤에 소리치고 있니?

8 The ants can't _________________ the stone.
그 개미들은 그 돌멩이를 옮길 수 없다.

Day 02 사물 묘사

01 empty
[émpti]

형 비어 있는, 빈
There is an empty nest on the branch.
나뭇가지 위에 빈 둥지가 있다.

02 gas
[gæs]

명 기체, 가스
We cannot see a gas like oxygen.
우리는 산소와 같은 기체를 볼 수 없다.

03 hard
[hɑːrd]

형 단단한, 딱딱한
The dog is digging in the hard ground.
그 개는 단단한 땅을 파고 있다.

04 heavy
[hévi]

형 무거운
A little boy lifted a heavy bag.
작은 소년이 무거운 가방을 들어 올렸다.

05 humid
[hjúːmid]

형 습한
It's really humid on a rainy day.
비 오는 날에는 정말 습하다.

06 light
[lait]

형 가벼운
Mom covered me with a light blanket.
엄마는 가벼운 이불로 나를 덮어 주셨다.

07 liquid
[líkwid]

명 액체 형 액체의
Use this liquid soap for washing your hands.
너의 손을 씻을 때 이 액체 비누를 사용해.

08 loose
[luːs]

형 헐거워진
A button on my shirt came loose.
나의 셔츠 단추가 헐거워졌다.

09 rough
[rʌf]

형 거친
The trunk has a rough surface.
그 나무의 몸통은 표면이 거칠다.

10 shallow
[ʃǽlou]

형 얕은
The fish can breathe in shallow water.
그 물고기는 얕은 물에서 숨을 쉴 수 있다.

Daily Test

A 우리말 뜻과 일치하도록 빠진 글자를 써넣어 단어를 완성하세요.

1 습한   __ u __ __ __

2 단단한, 딱딱한   __ __ r __

3 가벼운   __ __ g __ t

4 헐거워진   __ o __ __ e

5 비어 있는, 빈   __ __ p __ __

B 다음 영어 단어의 우리말 뜻을 쓰세요.

1 rough   _______________

2 gas   _______________

3 liquid   _______________

4 shallow   _______________

5 heavy   _______________

C 우리말 뜻과 일치하도록 빈칸에 알맞은 단어를 써넣어 문장을 완성하세요.

1 Use this _______________ soap for washing your hands.
너의 손을 씻을 때 이 액체 비누를 사용해.

2 A button on my shirt came _______________.
나의 셔츠 단추가 헐거워졌다.

3 A little boy lifted a _______________ bag.
작은 소년이 무거운 가방을 들어 올렸다.

4 We cannot see a _______________ like oxygen.
우리는 산소와 같은 기체를 볼 수 없다.

5 Mom covered me with a _______________ blanket.
엄마는 가벼운 이불로 나를 덮어 주셨다.

6 The fish can breathe in _______________ water.
그 물고기는 얕은 물에서 숨을 쉴 수 있다.

7 There is an _______________ nest on the branch.
나뭇가지 위에 빈 둥지가 있다.

8 It's really _______________ on a rainy day.
비 오는 날에는 정말 습하다.

11	**sharp** [ʃɑːrp]	형 날카로운, 뾰족한 You should use the sharp stick. 너희는 그 뾰족한 막대기를 사용하는 것이 좋겠다.
12	**smooth** [smuːð]	형 매끄러운, 매끈한 The silk dress is smooth. 그 실크 드레스는 매끄럽다.
13	**soft** [sɔ(ː)ft]	형 부드러운 Wipe your glasses with a soft cloth. 너의 안경을 부드러운 천으로 닦아.
14	**solid** [sάlid]	명 고체 형 단단한, 고체의 A solid has a fixed shape. 고체는 고정된 모양을 가지고 있다.
15	**steep** [stiːp]	형 가파른, 비탈진 Anna skied down the steep hill. Anna는 그 가파른 언덕을 스키를 타고 내려왔다.
16	**sticky** [stíki]	형 끈적거리는 My feet were sticky with sweat. 나의 발은 땀으로 끈적거렸다.
17	**thick** [θik]	형 두꺼운 I can hear his voice through the thick wall. 나는 그 두꺼운 벽을 통해 그의 목소리를 들을 수 있다.
18	**thin** [θin]	형 얇은, 마른 The board was as thin as this paper. 그 판자는 이 종이만큼 얇았다.
19	**tight** [tait]	형 꽉 조이는 The skirt is tight around the waist. 그 치마는 허리가 꽉 조인다.
20	**wet** [wet]	형 젖은 Take off your wet socks and shoes. 너의 젖은 양말과 신발을 벗어.

Daily Test

A 우리말 뜻과 일치하도록 빠진 글자를 써넣어 단어를 완성하세요.

1 젖은   __ e __

2 부드러운   __ __ __ t

3 두꺼운   t __ __ __ k

4 꽉 조이는   __ i g __ __

5 고체; 단단한, 고체의   __ o l __ __

B 다음 영어 단어의 우리말 뜻을 쓰세요.

1 smooth ________________

2 thin ________________

3 steep ________________

4 sharp ________________

5 sticky ________________

C 우리말 뜻과 일치하도록 빈칸에 알맞은 단어를 써넣어 문장을 완성하세요.

1 The skirt is ________________ around the waist.
그 치마는 허리가 꽉 조인다.

2 Anna skied down the ________________ hill.
Anna는 그 가파른 언덕을 스키를 타고 내려왔다.

3 A ________________ has a fixed shape.
고체는 고정된 모양을 가지고 있다.

4 Take off your ________________ socks and shoes.
너의 젖은 양말과 신발을 벗어.

5 You should use the ________________ stick.
너희는 그 뾰족한 막대기를 사용하는 것이 좋겠다.

6 My feet were ________________ with sweat.
나의 발은 땀으로 끈적거렸다.

7 The board was as ________________ as this paper.
그 판자는 이 종이만큼 얇았다.

8 I can hear his voice through the ________________ wall.
나는 그 두꺼운 벽을 통해 그의 목소리를 들을 수 있다.

01 ancient
[éinʃənt]

형 고대의
Ancient Greeks built this temple.
고대 그리스인들이 이 신전을 지었다.

02 classic
[klǽsik]

형 고전적인　명 고전, 명작
They used a classic design for the new car.
그들은 그 새로운 차에 고전적인 디자인을 사용했다.

03 comedy
[kάmidi]

명 코미디, 희극
They couldn't understand the comedy.
그들은 그 코미디를 이해하지 못했다.

04 copyright
[kάpiràit]

명 저작권
This magazine is protected by copyright.
이 잡지는 저작권에 의해 보호받는다.

05 culture
[kΛltʃər]

명 문화
Each country has its own culture.
각 나라는 그 나라만의 문화가 있다.

06 custom
[kΛstəm]

명 관습, 풍습
Bowing is a common custom here.
고개 숙여 인사하는 것은 여기에서는 흔한 관습이다.

07 different
[dífərənt]

형 다른
Let's think about this picture in a different way.
이 그림에 대해서 다른 방식으로 생각해 보자.

08 exhibition
[èksəbíʃən]

명 전시회
I got an invitation to the exhibition.
나는 그 전시회에 초대를 받았다.

09 fair
[fɛər]

명 박람회
We can see the invention in the fair.
우리는 그 박람회에서 그 발명품을 볼 수 있다.

10 festival
[féstəvəl]

명 축제
The festival includes fireworks.
그 축제는 불꽃놀이를 포함한다.

Daily Test

A 우리말 뜻과 일치하도록 빠진 글자를 써넣어 단어를 완성하세요.

1 박람회   _ _ _ r

2 고대의   _ n _ _ _ _ t

3 관습, 풍습   _ _ s _ o _

4 코미디, 희극   _ _ m e _ _

5 다른   d _ _ f _ _ _ n _

B 다음 영어 단어의 우리말 뜻을 쓰세요.

1 copyright   ___________

2 classic   ___________

3 festival   ___________

4 exhibition   ___________

5 culture   ___________

C 우리말 뜻과 일치하도록 빈칸에 알맞은 단어를 써넣어 문장을 완성하세요.

1 Each country has its own ___________.
각 나라는 그 나라만의 문화가 있다.

2 ___________ Greeks built this temple.
고대 그리스인들이 이 신전을 지었다.

3 We can see the invention in the ___________.
우리는 그 박람회에서 그 발명품을 볼 수 있다.

4 They couldn't understand the ___________.
그들은 그 코미디를 이해하지 못했다.

5 Let's think about this picture in a ___________ way.
이 그림에 대해서 다른 방식으로 생각해 보자.

6 I got an invitation to the ___________.
나는 그 전시회에 초대를 받았다.

7 This magazine is protected by ___________.
이 잡지는 저작권에 의해 보호받는다.

8 The ___________ includes fireworks.
그 축제는 불꽃놀이를 포함한다.

Day 03　문화

11 genre
[ʒɑ́:ŋrə]

명 장르
The genre of this book is science fiction.
이 책의 장르는 공상 과학이다.

12 modern
[mɑ́dərn]

형 현대의, 현대적인
Will you teach me about modern art?
나에게 현대 미술에 대해 가르쳐 줄래?

13 musical
[mjú:zikəl]

명 뮤지컬
The animation film was made into a musical.
그 만화 영화는 뮤지컬로 만들어졌다.

14 play
[plei]

명 희곡, 연극
Romeo and Juliet is a play by Shakespeare.
"로미오와 줄리엣"은 셰익스피어의 희곡이다.

15 show
[ʃou]

명 쇼
The show starts at 8 p.m.
그 쇼는 오후 8시에 시작한다.

16 similar
[símələr]

형 비슷한
Their lifestyle is similar to ours.
그들의 생활 방식은 우리의 것과 비슷하다.

17 stage
[steidʒ]

명 무대
Our seats are right in front of the stage.
우리의 좌석은 무대 바로 앞이다.

18 tradition
[trədíʃən]

명 전통
Eating noodles on a birthday is my family tradition.
생일에 국수를 먹는 것은 우리 가족의 전통이다.

19 tragedy
[trǽdʒidi]

명 비극
The story ends in tragedy.
그 이야기는 비극으로 끝난다.

20 various
[vέ(:)əriəs]

형 여러 가지의, 다양한
Judy is interested in various kinds of music.
Judy는 다양한 종류의 음악에 관심이 있다.

A 우리말 뜻과 일치하도록 빠진 글자를 써넣어 단어를 완성하세요.

1 현대의, 현대적인   __ __ d __ r __   2 뮤지컬   __ u __ __ c __ __

3 비극   __ __ __ g __ __ y   4 쇼   __ h __ __

5 장르   g __ n __ __

B 다음 영어 단어의 우리말 뜻을 쓰세요.

1 stage   _________________   2 play   _________________

3 various   _________________   4 tradition   _________________

5 similar   _________________

C 우리말 뜻과 일치하도록 빈칸에 알맞은 단어를 써넣어 문장을 완성하세요.

1 *Romeo and Juliet* is a _________________ by Shakespeare.
"로미오와 줄리엣"은 셰익스피어의 희곡이다.

2 The animation film was made into a _________________.
그 만화 영화는 뮤지컬로 만들어졌다.

3 Our seats are right in front of the _________________.
우리의 좌석은 무대 바로 앞이다.

4 The _________________ starts at 8 p.m.
그 쇼는 오후 8시에 시작한다.

5 The _________________ of this book is science fiction.
이 책의 장르는 공상 과학이다.

6 Eating noodles on a birthday is my family _________________.
생일에 국수를 먹는 것은 우리 가족의 전통이다.

7 Their lifestyle is _________________ to ours.
그들의 생활 방식은 우리의 것과 비슷하다.

8 The story ends in _________________.
그 이야기는 비극으로 끝난다.

 **Day 04** 정치

01 allow
[əláu]

⑧ 허락하다
They allowed us to import these goods.
그들은 우리가 이 상품들을 수입하는 것을 허락했다.

02 ban
[bæn]

⑧ 금지하다
The country will ban smoking in this area.
그 나라는 이 지역에서 흡연을 금지할 것이다.

03 campaign
[kæmpéin]

⑨ 캠페인
This is a campaign for energy saving.
이것은 에너지 절약을 위한 캠페인이다.

04 candidate
[kǽndidət]

⑨ 입후보자
All the candidates gathered together.
모든 후보자들이 함께 모였다.

05 civil
[sívəl]

⑩ 시민의
We are talking about civil rights.
우리는 시민권에 대해서 이야기하고 있다.

06 control
[kəntróul]

⑨ 지배, 통제 ⑧ 지배하다, 통제하다
The island is under the control of the army.
그 섬은 군대의 지배 아래에 있다.

07 democracy
[dimάkrəsi]

⑨ 민주주의
The students learned about democracy today.
그 학생들은 오늘 민주주의에 대해서 배웠다.

08 elect
[ilékt]

⑧ 선출하다
She was elected chairman.
그녀는 의장으로 선출되었다.

09 election
[ilékʃən]

⑨ 선거
The election will be held next Wednesday.
그 선거는 다음 수요일에 실시될 것이다.

10 government
[gʌ́vərnmənt]

⑨ 정부
The government promised to cut taxes.
정부는 세금을 줄이기로 약속했다.

Daily Test

A 우리말 뜻과 일치하도록 빠진 글자를 써넣어 단어를 완성하세요.

1 시민의   c __ __ i __

2 금지하다   __ __ n

3 허락하다   __ l __ __ w

4 선거   __ __ e c __ i __ __

5 캠페인   __ __ m __ __ __ g __

B 다음 영어 단어의 우리말 뜻을 쓰세요.

1 candidate   ___________________

2 democracy   ___________________

3 government   ___________________

4 elect   ___________________

5 control   ___________________

C 우리말 뜻과 일치하도록 빈칸에 알맞은 단어를 써넣어 문장을 완성하세요.

1 The students learned about _________________ today.
그 학생들은 오늘 민주주의에 대해서 배웠다.

2 We are talking about _________________ rights.
우리는 시민권에 대해서 이야기하고 있다.

3 The country will _________________ smoking in this area.
그 나라는 이 지역에서 흡연을 금지할 것이다.

4 The island is under the _________________ of the army.
그 섬은 군대의 지배 아래에 있다.

5 The _________________ will be held next Wednesday.
그 선거는 다음 수요일에 실시될 것이다.

6 All the _________________ gathered together.
모든 후보자들이 함께 모였다.

7 The _________________ promised to cut taxes.
정부는 세금을 줄이기로 약속했다.

8 This is a _________________ for energy saving.
이것은 에너지 절약을 위한 캠페인이다.

11 king
[kiŋ]

명 왕
Some countries still have a king.
몇몇 나라들에는 아직도 왕이 있다.

12 law
[lɔ:]

명 법
Did the company break the law?
그 회사는 법을 어겼니?

13 mayor
[méiər]

명 시장
He became the mayor of the city.
그는 그 도시의 시장이 되었다.

14 obey
[oubéi]

동 따르다
We won't obey his order.
우리는 그의 명령을 따르지 않을 것이다.

15 policy
[pálisi]

명 정책
She refused to follow the new policy.
그녀는 그 새로운 정책에 따르는 것을 거부했다.

16 politician
[pàlitíʃən]

명 정치인
I will interview the politician.
나는 그 정치인을 인터뷰할 것이다.

17 president
[prézidənt]

명 대통령
The president visited Asia yesterday.
그 대통령은 어제 아시아를 방문했다.

18 queen
[kwi:n]

명 여왕
The queen is loved by many people.
그 여왕은 많은 사람들에게 사랑받는다.

19 rule
[ru:l]

명 규칙, 통치   동 통치하다
He ruled the kingdom for ten years.
그는 그 왕국을 10년 동안 통치했다.

20 vote
[vout]

명 표, 투표   동 투표하다
Many young people will vote for the first time.
많은 젊은 사람들이 처음으로 투표할 것이다.

Daily Test

A 우리말 뜻과 일치하도록 빠진 글자를 써넣어 단어를 완성하세요.

1 정책   __ o __ __ __ y   **2** 여왕   __ __ e __ n

3 시장   __ __ y o __   **4** 법   __ a __

5 따르다   __ b __ __

B 다음 영어 단어의 우리말 뜻을 쓰세요.

1 vote _________________   **2** rule _________________

3 king _________________   **4** president _________________

5 politician _________________

C 우리말 뜻과 일치하도록 빈칸에 알맞은 단어를 써넣어 문장을 완성하세요.

1 Did the company break the _________________?
그 회사는 법을 어겼니?

2 The _________________ is loved by many people.
그 여왕은 많은 사람들에게 사랑받는다.

3 He became the _________________ of the city.
그는 그 도시의 시장이 되었다.

4 Some countries still have a _________________.
몇몇 나라들에는 아직도 왕이 있다.

5 The _________________ visited Asia yesterday.
그 대통령은 어제 아시아를 방문했다.

6 Many young people will _________________ for the first time.
많은 젊은 사람들이 처음으로 투표할 것이다.

7 I will interview the _________________.
나는 그 정치인을 인터뷰할 것이다.

8 He _________________ the kingdom for ten years.
그는 그 왕국을 10년 동안 통치했다.

A 우리말 뜻에 해당하는 영어 단어를 찾아 동그라미 하세요.

| 헐거워진 | 타다 | 박람회 | 두꺼운 | 시민의 |
| 건너다 | 희곡, 연극 | 무거운 | 쇼 | 규칙, 통치; 통치하다 |

r	f	s	h	o	w	r	j	t	k
c	i	v	d	k	j	b	n	h	c
r	x	d	h	h	z	f	a	i	r
c	v	h	e	a	v	y	j	c	o
i	x	f	n	q	l	g	n	k	s
v	j	p	l	a	y	j	x	j	s
i	u	t	c	d	f	q	k	k	w
l	o	o	s	e	q	r	u	l	e

B 우리말 뜻과 일치하도록 알맞은 단어를 골라 문장을 완성하세요.

| hard | action | elected | repairs | president | classic |

1 She was ________________ chairman.
그녀는 의장으로 선출되었다.

2 The hotel needs some ________________, doesn't it?
그 호텔은 수리가 필요해, 그렇지 않니?

3 They used a ________________ design for the new car.
그들은 그 새로운 차에 고전적인 디자인을 사용했다.

4 We really admire your brave ________________.
우리는 너의 용감한 행동을 정말 존경한다.

5 The dog is digging in the ________________ ground.
그 개는 단단한 땅을 파고 있다.

6 The ________________ visited Asia yesterday.
그 대통령은 어제 아시아를 방문했다.

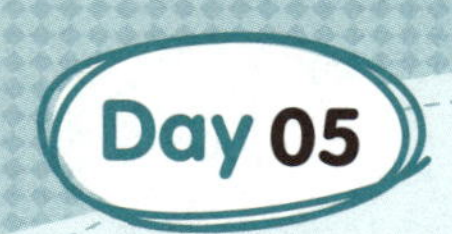

C 들려 주는 영어 단어를 바르게 쓴 다음, 우리말 뜻을 써넣으세요.

Day 05_C

	영어 단어	우리말		영어 단어	우리말
1			11		
2			12		
3			13		
4			14		
5			15		
6			16		
7			17		
8			18		
9			19		
10			20		

D 우리말 뜻과 일치하도록 알맞은 단어를 골라 동그라미 하세요.

1. The trunk has a (hard / rough) surface.
그 나무의 몸통은 표면이 거칠다.

2. She refused to follow the new (policy / government).
그녀는 그 새로운 정책에 따르는 것을 거부했다.

3. Will you teach me about (similar / modern) art?
나에게 현대 미술에 대해 가르쳐 줄래?

4. The silk dress is (smooth / tight).
그 실크 드레스는 매끄럽다.

5. I need to (leave / arrive) home soon.
나는 곧 집에서 출발해야 한다.

6. Bowing is a common (custom / copyright) here.
고개 숙여 인사하는 것은 여기에서는 흔한 관습이다.

E 영어는 우리말로, 우리말은 영어로 바꿔 쓰세요.

1	sticky	_______________	2	걷다, 걸어가다
3	activity	_______________	4	캠페인
5	tradition	_______________	6	코미디, 희극
7	control	_______________	8	나르다
9	humid	_______________	10	여왕
11	government	_______________	12	젖은
13	mayor	_______________	14	액체; 액체의
15	different	_______________	16	장르
17	move	_______________	18	뮤지컬
19	solid	_______________	20	운전하다

Day 05_F

F 잘 듣고, 빈칸에 알맞은 단어를 써넣어 문장을 완성하세요.

1 Did the company break the _______________?

2 I got an invitation to the _______________.

3 There is an _______________ nest on the branch.

4 He is _______________ on the table with his hands.

5 They _______________ us to import these goods.

6 Please show your ticket before you _______________.

7 Wipe your glasses with a _______________ cloth.

8 Our seats are right in front of the _______________.

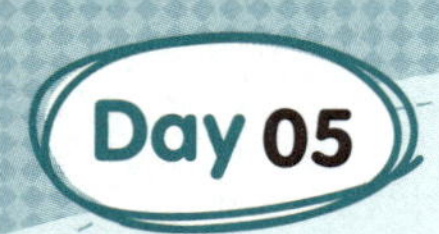

Day 05

G 우리말 뜻과 일치하도록 빈칸에 알맞은 단어를 써넣어 문장을 완성하세요.

1 She ran fast to a________________ on time.
그녀는 제시간에 도착하기 위해 빠르게 달렸다.

2 I will interview the p________________.
나는 그 정치인을 인터뷰할 것이다.

3 Each country has its own c________________.
각 나라는 그 나라만의 문화가 있다.

4 Why are they s________________ at night?
그들은 왜 밤에 소리치고 있니?

5 The students learned about d________________ today.
그 학생들은 오늘 민주주의에 대해서 배웠다.

6 The fish can breathe in s________________ water.
그 물고기는 얕은 물에서 숨을 쉴 수 있다.

7 The kid is able to c________________ to 100.
그 아이는 100까지 셀 수 있다.

8 Judy is interested in v________________ kinds of music.
Judy는 다양한 종류의 음악에 관심이 있다.

9 We won't o________________ his order.
우리는 그의 명령을 따르지 않을 것이다.

10 The skirt is t________________ around the waist.
그 치마는 허리가 꽉 조인다.

Review에서 틀린 문제의 영어 단어와 우리말 뜻을 쓴 다음, 영어 단어를 3번씩 쓰세요.

	( )	________ ________ ________
	( )	________ ________ ________
	( )	________ ________ ________
	( )	________ ________ ________
	( )	________ ________ ________

01 bay
[bei]
명 (바다의) 만
That bridge crosses the bay.
저 다리는 그 만을 가로지른다.

02 beach
[bi:tʃ]
명 해변, 바닷가
The women are singing at the beach.
그 여자들은 해변에서 노래를 부르고 있다.

03 cave
[keiv]
명 동굴
It is the largest cave in the world.
그것은 세상에서 가장 큰 동굴이다.

04 cliff
[klif]
명 절벽
The sign says to stay away from the cliff.
그 표지판에는 절벽에서 떨어져 있으라고 쓰여 있다.

05 coast
[koust]
명 해안
There are some houses along the coast.
해안을 따라 집들이 있다.

06 desert
[dézərt]
명 사막
The desert is cold at night.
그 사막은 밤에 춥다.

07 environment
[inváiərənmənt]
명 환경
Our main concern is the environment.
우리의 주된 관심사는 환경이다.

08 field
[fi:ld]
명 들판
Are they catching grasshoppers in the field?
그들은 들판에서 메뚜기들을 잡고 있니?

09 forest
[fɔ́(:)rist]
명 숲
Did you enjoy hiking in the forest?
너희는 숲에서 하이킹을 즐겼니?

10 ground
[graund]
명 땅바닥, 땅
A turtle is crawling on the ground.
거북 한 마리가 땅 위를 기어가고 있다.

Daily Test

A 우리말 뜻과 일치하도록 빠진 글자를 써넣어 단어를 완성하세요.

1 땅바닥, 땅   __ __ o __ n __

2 사막   __ e __ e __ __

3 동굴   __ a __ __

4 해변, 바닷가   b __ __ c __

5 들판   __ i __ l __

B 다음 영어 단어의 우리말 뜻을 쓰세요.

1 bay   **2** cliff

3 environment   **4** forest

5 coast

C 우리말 뜻과 일치하도록 빈칸에 알맞은 단어를 써넣어 문장을 완성하세요.

1 Are they catching grasshoppers in the _________________?
그들은 들판에서 메뚜기들을 잡고 있니?

2 The _________________ is cold at night.
그 사막은 밤에 춥다.

3 The sign says to stay away from the _________________.
그 표지판에는 절벽에서 떨어져 있으라고 쓰여 있다.

4 The women are singing at the _________________.
그 여자들은 해변에서 노래를 부르고 있다.

5 It is the largest _________________ in the world.
그것은 세상에서 가장 큰 동굴이다.

6 Did you enjoy hiking in the _________________?
너희는 숲에서 하이킹을 즐겼니?

7 Our main concern is the _________________.
우리의 주된 관심사는 환경이다.

8 There are some houses along the _________________.
해안을 따라 집들이 있다.

11 hill
[hil]

명 언덕

White clouds are floating over the hill.
하얀 구름들이 언덕 위로 떠가고 있다.

12 island
[áilənd]

명 섬

It takes one hour to go to the island by ship.
배로 그 섬까지 가는 데에는 1시간이 걸린다.

13 jungle
[dʒʌ́ŋgl]

명 밀림, 정글

Many unknown insects live in the jungle.
많은 알려지지 않은 곤충들이 정글에 산다.

14 mountain
[máuntən]

명 산

I saw the sunrise on the top of the mountain.
나는 산꼭대기에서 일출을 봤다.

15 rock
[rɑk]

명 바위

We found some shellfish under the rock.
우리는 바위 아래에서 조개류를 발견했다.

16 sand
[sænd]

명 모래

The kids are filling the bucket with sand.
그 아이들은 그 양동이를 모래로 채우고 있다.

17 sea
[si:]

명 바다

Peter can dive into the deep sea.
Peter는 깊은 바닷속으로 다이빙할 수 있다.

18 soil
[sɔil]

명 흙, 토양

It is time to change the soil in the pot.
화분에 있는 흙을 바꿀 때이다.

19 stream
[stri:m]

명 개울, 시내

Let's sit down near the stream!
개울 근처에 앉자!

20 wave
[weiv]

명 파도

Big waves hit the boat last night.
큰 파도가 어젯밤 배를 강타했다.

Daily Test

A 우리말 뜻과 일치하도록 빠진 글자를 써넣어 단어를 완성하세요.

1 바다   __ __ a   **2** 밀림, 정글   __ __ n __ l __

3 파도   __ a __ __   **4** 바위   __ __ c __

5 섬   __ __ l __ n __

B 다음 영어 단어의 우리말 뜻을 쓰세요.

1 stream   _________________   **2** hill   _________________

3 soil   _________________   **4** sand   _________________

5 mountain   _________________

C 우리말 뜻과 일치하도록 빈칸에 알맞은 단어를 써넣어 문장을 완성하세요.

1 I saw the sunrise on the top of the _________________.
나는 산꼭대기에서 일출을 봤다.

2 Many unknown insects live in the _________________.
많은 알려지지 않은 곤충들이 정글에 산다.

3 Let's sit down near the _________________!
개울 근처에 앉자!

4 Peter can dive into the deep _________________.
Peter는 깊은 바닷속으로 다이빙할 수 있다.

5 White clouds are floating over the _________________.
하얀 구름들이 언덕 위로 떠가고 있다.

6 The kids are filling the bucket with _________________.
그 아이들은 그 양동이를 모래로 채우고 있다.

7 It takes one hour to go to the _________________ by ship.
배로 그 섬까지 가는 데에는 1시간이 걸린다.

8 We found some shellfish under the _________________.
우리는 바위 아래에서 조개류를 발견했다.

01 amazing
[əméiziŋ]

형 놀라운
The study shows amazing results.
그 연구는 놀라운 결과를 보여 준다.

02 available
[əvéiləbl]

형 이용할 수 있는, 시간이 있는
The library is available from 10 a.m. to 10 p.m.
그 도서관은 오전 10시부터 오후 10시까지 이용할 수 있다.

03 boring
[bɔ́:riŋ]

형 지루한
The basketball game was pretty boring.
그 농구 경기는 꽤 지루했다.

04 brief
[bri:f]

형 짧은, 간단한
The expert sent a brief answer to us.
그 전문가는 우리에게 짧은 답변을 보냈다.

05 confusing
[kənfjú:ziŋ]

형 혼란스러운
I received a very confusing message.
나는 매우 혼란스러운 메시지를 받았다.

06 disappointing
[dìsəpɔ́intiŋ]

형 실망스러운
Today was a disappointing day.
오늘은 실망스러운 날이었다.

07 effective
[iféktiv]

형 효과적인
The new system is highly effective.
그 새로운 시스템은 매우 효과적이다.

08 entire
[intáiər]

형 전체의
Do you understand the entire process?
너는 그 전체 과정을 이해하니?

09 exciting
[iksáitiŋ]

형 신나는, 흥미진진한
The car race will be exciting.
그 자동차 경주는 흥미진진할 것이다.

10 interesting
[íntərəstiŋ]

형 재미있는, 흥미로운
The college offers many interesting classes.
그 대학은 많은 재미있는 수업들을 제공한다.

Daily Test

A 우리말 뜻과 일치하도록 빠진 글자를 써넣어 단어를 완성하세요.

1 전체의   __ __ t __ r __

2 혼란스러운   __ __ __ f __ s __ __ __ __

3 지루한   __ o __ __ __ g

4 효과적인   __ __ f __ c __ __ v __

5 놀라운   a __ __ z __ __ __ __

B 다음 영어 단어의 우리말 뜻을 쓰세요.

1 interesting   __________________

2 brief   __________________

3 exciting   __________________

4 available   __________________

5 disappointing   __________________

C 우리말 뜻과 일치하도록 빈칸에 알맞은 단어를 써넣어 문장을 완성하세요.

1 Today was a __________________ day.
오늘은 실망스러운 날이었다.

2 I received a very __________________ message.
나는 매우 혼란스러운 메시지를 받았다.

3 The college offers many __________________ classes.
그 대학은 많은 재미있는 수업들을 제공한다.

4 The car race will be __________________.
그 자동차 경주는 흥미진진할 것이다.

5 Do you understand the __________________ process?
너는 그 전체 과정을 이해하니?

6 The library is __________________ from 10 a.m. to 10 p.m.
그 도서관은 오전 10시부터 오후 10시까지 이용할 수 있다.

7 The new system is highly __________________.
그 새로운 시스템은 매우 효과적이다.

8 The basketball game was pretty __________________.
그 농구 경기는 꽤 지루했다.

11 normal [nɔ́ːrməl]
형 보통의, 평범한, 정상적인
It's normal to feel sad about the news.
그 소식에 슬퍼하는 것은 정상이다.

12 particular [pərtíkjələr]
형 특정한, 특별한
I'm looking for a particular book on Europe.
나는 유럽에 대한 특정한 책을 찾고 있다.

13 possible [pásəbl]
형 가능한
Is it possible to enter the old temple?
그 낡은 절에 들어가는 것은 가능하니?

14 related [riléitid]
형 관련된   ✿ related to ~와 관련된
Is this information related to him?
이 정보는 그와 관련된 것이니?

15 serious [sí(ː)əriəs]
형 심각한, 진지한
School violence is a serious problem.
학교 폭력은 심각한 문제이다.

16 suddenly [sʌ́dnli]
부 갑자기
Why did she cancel the project suddenly?
그녀는 왜 갑자기 그 프로젝트를 취소했니?

17 sure [ʃuər]
형 확신하는
Are you sure about that?
너는 그것에 대해서 확신하니?

18 surprising [sərpráiziŋ]
형 놀라운
I have more surprising news.
나에게 더 놀라운 소식이 있다.

19 urgent [ə́ːrdʒənt]
형 긴급한
He called an urgent meeting this morning.
그는 오늘 아침 긴급 회의를 소집했다.

20 worth [wəːrθ]
형 ~할 가치가 있는
This book is worth reading.
이 책은 읽을 가치가 있다.

Daily Test

A 우리말 뜻과 일치하도록 빠진 글자를 써넣어 단어를 완성하세요.

1 가능한   _ _ s _ i _ _ _   **2** 심각한, 진지한   _ _ r _ _ _ s

3 관련된   _ e _ _ _ e _   **4** 긴급한   _ r g _ _ _ _

5 ~할 가치가 있는   _ o _ t _

B 다음 영어 단어의 우리말 뜻을 쓰세요.

1 sure   _________________   **2** suddenly   _________________

3 normal   _________________   **4** particular   _________________

5 surprising   _________________

C 우리말 뜻과 일치하도록 빈칸에 알맞은 단어를 써넣어 문장을 완성하세요.

1 Why did she cancel the project _________________?
그녀는 왜 갑자기 그 프로젝트를 취소했니?

2 I'm looking for a _________________ book on Europe.
나는 유럽에 대한 특정한 책을 찾고 있다.

3 School violence is a _________________ problem.
학교 폭력은 심각한 문제이다.

4 It's _________________ to feel sad about the news.
그 소식에 슬퍼하는 것은 정상이다.

5 Is this information _________________ to him?
이 정보는 그와 관련된 것이니?

6 Are you _________________ about that?
너는 그것에 대해서 확신하니?

7 He called an _________________ meeting this morning.
그는 오늘 아침 긴급 회의를 소집했다.

8 Is it _________________ to enter the old temple?
그 낡은 절에 들어가는 것은 가능하니?

01 consist
[kənsíst]

동 구성되다 ✿ consist of ~로 구성되다
A human body consists of cells.
인체는 세포들로 구성되어 있다.

02 contain
[kəntéin]

동 ~이 들어 있다
How much salt does sea water contain?
바닷물에는 얼마나 많은 소금이 들어 있니?

03 discover
[diskʌ́vər]

동 발견하다
She discovered a rare species of bird.
그녀는 희귀한 종의 새를 발견했다.

04 earth
[ə:rθ]

명 지구
Who first said the earth is round?
누가 지구가 둥글다고 처음 말했니?

05 element
[éləmənt]

명 요소, 원소
Oxygen is a chemical element.
산소는 화학 원소이다.

06 examine
[igzǽmin]

동 조사하다, 검토하다
He is examining the data on global warming.
그는 지구 온난화에 대한 자료를 검토하고 있다.

07 example
[igzǽmpl]

명 예, 사례
Could you tell me an example of the errors?
그 오류들 중 한 예를 말해 줄 수 있나요?

08 experiment
[ikspérəmənt]

명 실험 동 실험하다
The students did an experiment on animals.
그 학생들은 동물에 관한 실험을 했다.

09 explore
[ikspló:r]

동 탐험하다, 탐사하다
David wants to explore Mars someday.
David는 언젠가 화성을 탐사하기를 원한다.

10 find
[faind]

동 찾다, 찾아내다 ✿ find-found-found
He found two dinosaur fossils.
그는 공룡 화석 두 개를 찾아냈다.

Daily Test

A 우리말 뜻과 일치하도록 빠진 글자를 써넣어 단어를 완성하세요.

1 지구   __ __ r __ h

2 탐험하다, 탐사하다   __ __ p __ __ r __

3 예, 사례   __ x __ __ __ l __

4 찾다, 찾아내다   __ __ __ d

5 구성되다   __ __ __ s __ s __

B 다음 영어 단어의 우리말 뜻을 쓰세요.

1 element   __________________

2 contain   __________________

3 experiment   __________________

4 discover   __________________

5 examine   __________________

C 우리말 뜻과 일치하도록 빈칸에 알맞은 단어를 써넣어 문장을 완성하세요.

1 Who first said the __________________ is round?
누가 지구가 둥글다고 처음 말했니?

2 How much salt does sea water __________________?
바닷물에는 얼마나 많은 소금이 들어 있니?

3 David wants to __________________ Mars someday.
David는 언젠가 화성을 탐사하기를 원한다.

4 He is __________________ the data on global warming.
그는 지구 온난화에 대한 자료를 검토하고 있다.

5 The students did an __________________ on animals.
그 학생들은 동물에 관한 실험을 했다.

6 Oxygen is a chemical __________________.
산소는 화학 원소이다.

7 Could you tell me an __________________ of the errors?
그 오류들 중 한 예를 말해 줄 수 있나요?

8 A human body __________________ of cells.
인체는 세포들로 구성되어 있다.

 **Day 08** 우주와 과학

11 gravity
[grǽvəti]

명 중력
We can stand on the ground thanks to gravity.
우리는 중력 덕분에 땅 위에 설 수 있다.

12 lab
[læb]

명 실험실
I am studying the new medicine in the lab.
나는 실험실에서 그 새로운 약을 연구하고 있다.

13 magnet
[mǽgnit]

명 자석
Those clips can stick to magnets.
저 클립들은 자석에 붙을 수 있다.

14 method
[méθəd]

명 방법
Let's try this method again.
이 방법을 다시 시도해 보자.

15 moon
[mu:n]

명 달 ✿ full moon 보름달
We can see a full moon tonight.
우리는 오늘 밤 보름달을 볼 수 있다.

16 planet
[plǽnit]

명 행성
Some planets have rings around them.
어떤 행성들은 그 주위에 고리들이 있다.

17 space
[speis]

명 우주
The astronauts are returning from space.
그 우주 비행사들이 우주에서 돌아오고 있다.

18 star
[stɑːr]

명 별
Which is the brightest star in the sky?
하늘에서 가장 밝은 별은 어느 것이니?

19 sun
[sʌn]

명 해, 태양
What time did the sun set?
해가 몇 시에 졌니?

20 universe
[júːnəvə̀ːrs]

명 우주, 은하계
How was the universe created?
우주는 어떻게 만들어졌니?

Daily Test

A 우리말 뜻과 일치하도록 빠진 글자를 써넣어 단어를 완성하세요.

1 자석   __ a __ __ e __   **2** 우주   s __ a __ __

3 행성   __ l __ __ __ t   **4** 달   __ __ o __

5 중력   __ __ __ v __ t __

B 다음 영어 단어의 우리말 뜻을 쓰세요.

1 star   ________________   **2** universe   ________________

3 lab   ________________   **4** sun   ________________

5 method   ________________

C 우리말 뜻과 일치하도록 빈칸에 알맞은 단어를 써넣어 문장을 완성하세요.

1 We can see a full ________________ tonight.
우리는 오늘 밤 보름달을 볼 수 있다.

2 Let's try this ________________ again.
이 방법을 다시 시도해 보자.

3 Those clips can stick to ________________.
저 클립들은 자석에 붙을 수 있다.

4 Which is the brightest ________________ in the sky?
하늘에서 가장 밝은 별은 어느 것이니?

5 Some ________________ have rings around them.
어떤 행성들은 그 주위에 고리들이 있다.

6 What time did the ________________ set?
해가 몇 시에 졌니?

7 We can stand on the ground thanks to ________________.
우리는 중력 덕분에 땅 위에 설 수 있다.

8 I am studying the new medicine in the ________________.
나는 실험실에서 그 새로운 약을 연구하고 있다.

01 account
[əkáunt]

명 계좌

I opened my first bank account yesterday.
나는 어제 나의 첫 은행 계좌를 만들었다.

02 bill
[bil]

명 지폐

Can I change this bill into coins?
이 지폐를 동전으로 바꿀 수 있을까요?

03 borrow
[bárou]

동 빌리다

She had to borrow 5 dollars from her friend.
그녀는 그녀의 친구에게 5달러를 빌려야 했다.

04 budget
[bʌ́dʒit]

명 예산

What is your monthly budget?
너의 한 달 예산은 얼마나 되니?

05 charge
[tʃɑːrdʒ]

동 (요금을) 청구하다 명 요금

The restaurant charged $10 for ice.
그 식당은 얼음 값으로 10달러를 청구했다.

06 debt
[det]

명 빚

I paid my debts without anyone's help.
나는 누구의 도움도 받지 않고 나의 빚을 갚았다.

07 earn
[əːrn]

동 벌다

Ellen earns 30,000 dollars a year.
Ellen은 1년에 3만 달러를 번다.

08 economy
[ikánəmi]

명 경제

The world economy is getting better.
세계 경제가 좋아지고 있다.

09 exchange
[ikstʃéindʒ]

동 교환하다 명 교환

Could you exchange this camera?
이 카메라를 교환해 줄 수 있나요?

10 expense
[ikspéns]

명 비용

The company will cover all the expenses.
그 회사가 모든 비용을 부담할 것이다.

Daily Test

A 우리말 뜻과 일치하도록 빠진 글자를 써넣어 단어를 완성하세요.

1 예산　　　__ __ d __ e __

2 지폐　　　__ __ __ l

3 비용　　　__ __ p __ __ s __

4 빌리다　　__ __ r __ __ w

5 계좌　　　__ c __ __ u __ __

B 다음 영어 단어의 우리말 뜻을 쓰세요.

1 charge　　________________

2 economy　________________

3 exchange　________________

4 debt　　　________________

5 earn　　　________________

C 우리말 뜻과 일치하도록 빈칸에 알맞은 단어를 써넣어 문장을 완성하세요.

1 What is your monthly ________________?
너의 한 달 예산은 얼마나 되니?

2 I opened my first bank ________________ yesterday.
나는 어제 나의 첫 은행 계좌를 만들었다.

3 Could you ________________ this camera?
이 카메라를 교환해 줄 수 있나요?

4 The restaurant ________________ $10 for ice.
그 식당은 얼음 값으로 10달러를 청구했다.

5 Ellen ________________ 30,000 dollars a year.
Ellen은 1년에 3만 달러를 번다.

6 Can I change this ________________ into coins?
이 지폐를 동전으로 바꿀 수 있을까요?

7 She had to ________________ 5 dollars from her friend.
그녀는 그녀의 친구에게 5달러를 빌려야 했다.

8 The world ________________ is getting better.
세계 경제가 좋아지고 있다.

11 export
[동 ikspɔ́ːrt 명 ékspɔːrt]

동 수출하다　명 수출
His roses are exported abroad.
그의 장미는 해외로 수출된다.

12 import
[동 impɔ́ːrt 명 ímpɔːrt]

동 수입하다　명 수입
They import tropical fruits from Thailand.
그들은 태국에서 열대 과일을 수입한다.

13 invest
[invést]

동 투자하다
She invested in the new business.
그녀는 그 새로운 사업에 투자했다.

14 lend
[lend]

동 빌려 주다　✿ lend-lent-lent
Can you lend me 15 dollars?
나에게 15달러를 빌려 줄 수 있니?

15 money
[mʌ́ni]

명 돈
I don't have enough money to buy it.
나는 그것을 살 만큼 충분한 돈이 없다.

16 poor
[puər]

형 가난한
The carpenter fixes the poor family's house.
그 목수는 그 가난한 가족의 집을 수리한다.

17 price
[prais]

명 값, 가격
The store was selling the shoes at half price.
그 가게는 신발들을 반값에 팔고 있었다.

18 rich
[ritʃ]

형 부유한
The rich man donates 10,000 dollars every year.
그 부유한 남자는 매년 10,000달러를 기부한다.

19 spend
[spend]

동 쓰다, 소비하다　✿ spend-spent-spent
How much do you spend a week?
너는 일주일에 얼마를 쓰니?

20 tax
[tæks]

명 세금
Why will the government raise taxes?
정부는 왜 세금을 올릴 건가요?

Daily Test

A 우리말 뜻과 일치하도록 빠진 글자를 써넣어 단어를 완성하세요.

1 가난한   __ __ __ r   **2** 빌려 주다   __ __ n __

3 수출하다; 수출   __ __ __ o __ t   **4** 값, 가격   __ r __ __ e

5 돈   m __ __ e __

B 다음 영어 단어의 우리말 뜻을 쓰세요.

1 invest   ________________   **2** spend   ________________

3 tax   ________________   **4** import   ________________

5 rich   ________________

C 우리말 뜻과 일치하도록 빈칸에 알맞은 단어를 써넣어 문장을 완성하세요.

1 She ________________ in the new business.
그녀는 그 새로운 사업에 투자했다.

2 They ________________ tropical fruits from Thailand.
그들은 태국에서 열대 과일을 수입한다.

3 The store was selling the shoes at half ________________.
그 가게는 신발들을 반값에 팔고 있었다.

4 How much do you ________________ a week?
너는 일주일에 얼마를 쓰니?

5 His roses are ________________ abroad.
그의 장미는 해외로 수출된다.

6 The carpenter fixes the ________________ family's house.
그 목수는 그 가난한 가족의 집을 수리한다.

7 I don't have enough ________________ to buy it.
나는 그것을 살 만큼 충분한 돈이 없다.

8 The ________________ man donates 10,000 dollars every year.
그 부유한 남자는 매년 10,000달러를 기부한다.

A 우리말 뜻에 해당하는 영어 단어를 찾아 동그라미 하세요.

별	바위	전체의	파도	확신하는
동굴	지구	지폐	부유한	빛

e	b	i	l	l	s	u	r	e	g
n	l	s	m	z	t	s	m	a	b
t	l	n	t	d	a	n	k	r	r
i	t	b	n	e	r	m	s	t	i
r	m	g	e	b	t	c	b	h	c
e	w	v	t	t	p	l	a	j	h
f	a	c	p	y	n	h	p	v	g
w	s	l	r	o	c	k	g	g	e

B 우리말 뜻과 일치하도록 알맞은 단어를 골라 문장을 완성하세요.

worth	coast	brief	found	universe	expenses

1 He ___________________ two dinosaur fossils.
그는 공룡 화석 두 개를 찾아냈다.

2 There are some houses along the ________________.
해안을 따라 집들이 있다.

3 The company will cover all the ________________.
그 회사가 모든 비용을 부담할 것이다.

4 The expert sent a ________________ answer to us.
그 전문가는 우리에게 짧은 답변을 보냈다.

5 How was the ________________ created?
우주는 어떻게 만들어졌니?

6 This book is ________________ reading.
이 책은 읽을 가치가 있다.

Day 10

Day 10_C

C 들려 주는 영어 단어를 바르게 쓴 다음, 우리말 뜻을 써넣으세요.

	영어 단어	우리말		영어 단어	우리말
1			11		
2			12		
3			13		
4			14		
5			15		
6			16		
7			17		
8			18		
9			19		
10			20		

D 우리말 뜻과 일치하도록 알맞은 단어를 골라 동그라미 하세요.

1 She (explored / discovered) a rare species of bird.
그녀는 희귀한 종의 새를 발견했다.

2 That bridge crosses the (bay / cave).
저 다리는 그 만을 가로지른다.

3 Can you (spend / lend) me 15 dollars?
나에게 15달러를 빌려 줄 수 있니?

4 I have more (surprising / exciting) news.
나에게 더 놀라운 소식이 있다.

5 It is time to change the (sand / soil) in the pot.
화분에 있는 흙을 바꿀 때이다.

6 Ellen (earns / borrows) 30,000 dollars a year.
Ellen은 1년에 3만 달러를 번다.

1	sea	__________	2	가능한	__________
3	effective	__________	4	해변, 바닷가	__________
5	lab	__________	6	예, 사례	__________
7	desert	__________	8	경제	__________
9	planet	__________	10	방법	__________
11	element	__________	12	긴급한	__________
13	normal	__________	14	빌리다	__________
15	import	__________	16	숲	__________
17	jungle	__________	18	돈	__________
19	spend	__________	20	혼란스러운	__________

F 잘 듣고, 빈칸에 알맞은 단어를 써넣어 문장을 완성하세요.

Day 10_F

1 How much salt does sea water __________?

2 The restaurant __________ $10 for ice.

3 Our main concern is the __________.

4 Why will the government raise __________?

5 Is this information __________ to him?

6 The study shows __________ results.

7 It takes one hour to go to the __________ by ship.

8 The astronauts are returning from __________.

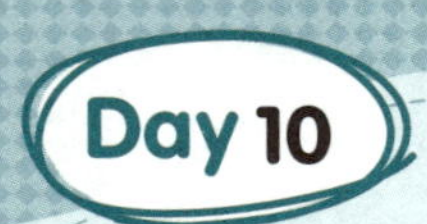

Day 10

 우리말 뜻과 일치하도록 빈칸에 알맞은 단어를 써넣어 문장을 완성하세요.

1 I opened my first bank a________________ yesterday.
나는 어제 나의 첫 은행 계좌를 만들었다.

2 I saw the sunrise on the top of the m________________.
나는 산꼭대기에서 일출을 봤다.

3 The students did an e________________ on animals.
그 학생들은 동물에 관한 실험을 했다.

4 His roses are e________________ abroad.
그의 장미는 해외로 수출된다.

5 The library is a________________ from 10 a.m. to 10 p.m.
그 도서관은 오전 10시부터 오후 10시까지 이용할 수 있다.

6 A turtle is crawling on the g________________.
거북 한 마리가 땅 위를 기어가고 있다.

7 Why did she cancel the project s________________?
그녀는 왜 갑자기 그 프로젝트를 취소했니?

8 The store was selling the shoes at half p________________.
그 가게는 신발들을 반값에 팔고 있었다.

9 We can stand on the ground thanks to g________________.
우리는 중력 덕분에 땅 위에 설 수 있다.

10 The college offers many i________________ classes.
그 대학은 많은 재미있는 수업들을 제공한다.

Review에서 틀린 문제의 영어 단어와 우리말 뜻을 쓴 다음, 영어 단어를 3번씩 쓰세요.

01	**achieve** [ətʃíːv]	통 성취하다 He practices hard to achieve his dream. 그는 그의 꿈을 성취하기 위해 열심히 연습한다.
02	**begin** [bigín]	통 시작하다, 시작되다　✿ begin-began-begun The Olympic Games will begin next week. 올림픽 대회는 다음 주에 시작될 것이다.
03	**case** [keis]	명 경우, 사례 In this case, ring the alarm bell first. 이런 경우에는, 먼저 비상벨을 울리세요.
04	**cause** [kɔːz]	명 원인　통 ~을 초래하다 What was the cause of the accident? 그 사고의 원인은 무엇이었니?
05	**check** [tʃek]	통 확인하다　명 확인 Did you check your e-mail this morning? 오늘 아침에 너의 이메일을 확인했니?
06	**complete** [kəmplíːt]	통 완료하다　형 완벽한 He completed the report in a day. 그는 그 보고서를 하루 만에 완료했다.
07	**continue** [kəntínju(ː)]	통 계속되다, 계속하다 They continued to talk after lunch. 그들은 점심 식사 후에 계속해서 이야기했다.
08	**delay** [diléi]	명 지연, 연기　통 연기하다 The train was delayed because of the heavy snow. 그 기차는 폭설 때문에 지연되었다.
09	**effect** [ifékt]	명 영향, 효과 The Internet has both good and bad effects. 인터넷은 좋은 영향과 나쁜 영향을 둘 다 가지고 있다.
10	**effort** [éfərt]	명 수고, 노력　✿ make an effort 노력하다 The doctor made an effort to cure her. 그 의사는 그녀를 치료하기 위해 노력했다.

Daily Test

A 우리말 뜻과 일치하도록 빠진 글자를 써넣어 단어를 완성하세요.

1 확인하다; 확인   __ h __ c __

2 영향, 효과   __ f f __ __ __ __

3 경우, 사례   __ __ s __

4 원인; ~을 초래하다   c __ u __ __

5 수고, 노력   __ __ f __ r __

B 다음 영어 단어의 우리말 뜻을 쓰세요.

1 continue   ________________

2 achieve   ________________

3 begin   ________________

4 delay   ________________

5 complete   ________________

C 우리말 뜻과 일치하도록 빈칸에 알맞은 단어를 써넣어 문장을 완성하세요.

1 The Olympic Games will ________________ next week.
올림픽 대회는 다음 주에 시작될 것이다.

2 He practices hard to ________________ his dream.
그는 그의 꿈을 성취하기 위해 열심히 연습한다.

3 They ________________ to talk after lunch.
그들은 점심 식사 후에 계속해서 이야기했다.

4 The train was ________________ because of the heavy snow.
그 기차는 폭설 때문에 지연되었다.

5 He ________________ the report in a day.
그는 그 보고서를 하루 만에 완료했다.

6 What was the ________________ of the accident?
그 사고의 원인은 무엇이었니?

7 The doctor made an ________________ to cure her.
그 의사는 그녀를 치료하기 위해 노력했다.

8 Did you ________________ your e-mail this morning?
오늘 아침에 너의 이메일을 확인했니?

11 encourage
[inkə́:ridʒ]

동 격려하다, 용기를 북돋우다
She **encouraged** him not to give up.
그녀는 그가 포기하지 않도록 격려했다.

12 fail
[feil]

동 실패하다
The girl is not afraid to **fail**.
그 소녀는 실패하는 것을 두려워하지 않는다.

13 finish
[fíniʃ]

동 끝내다, 끝나다 명 끝
I need three weeks to **finish** the work.
나는 그 일을 끝내려면 3주가 필요하다.

14 focus
[fóukəs]

동 집중하다 명 초점, 주목
Our store always **focuses** on the latest trend.
우리 가게는 항상 최신 유행에 집중한다.

15 goal
[goul]

명 목표
My **goal** is to renew my own record.
나의 목표는 나의 기록을 경신하는 것이다.

16 hurry
[hə́:ri]

동 서두르다, 급히 가다
Hurry up, or we'll be late for the show.
서둘러, 그러지 않으면 우리는 그 쇼에 늦을 거야.

17 important
[impɔ́:rtənt]

형 중요한
It was an **important** fact to me.
그것은 나에게 중요한 사실이었다.

18 process
[práses]

명 과정
Please explain the **process** in detail.
그 과정을 자세히 설명해 주세요.

19 result
[rizʌ́lt]

명 결과
He is waiting for the test **result**.
그는 시험 결과를 기다리고 있다.

20 succeed
[səksí:d]

동 성공하다
I'm sure that you will **succeed**.
나는 네가 성공할 것이라고 확신한다.

Daily Test

A 우리말 뜻과 일치하도록 빠진 글자를 써넣어 단어를 완성하세요.

1 결과   __ __ s __ __ t   **2** 목표   __ __ __ l

3 과정   __ r __ c __ __ __   **4** 실패하다   __ a __ __

5 집중하다; 초점, 주목   __ __ c __ s

B 다음 영어 단어의 우리말 뜻을 쓰세요.

1 finish   ________________   **2** important   ________________

3 succeed   ________________   **4** hurry   ________________

5 encourage   ________________

C 우리말 뜻과 일치하도록 빈칸에 알맞은 단어를 써넣어 문장을 완성하세요.

1 Please explain the ________________ in detail.
그 과정을 자세히 설명해 주세요.

2 I need three weeks to ________________ the work.
나는 그 일을 끝내려면 3주가 필요하다.

3 It was an ________________ fact to me.
그것은 나에게 중요한 사실이었다.

4 I'm sure that you will ________________.
나는 네가 성공할 것이라고 확신한다.

5 She ________________ him not to give up.
그녀는 그가 포기하지 않도록 격려했다.

6 Our store always ________________ on the latest trend.
우리 가게는 항상 최신 유행에 집중한다.

7 The girl is not afraid to ________________.
그 소녀는 실패하는 것을 두려워하지 않는다.

8 He is waiting for the test ________________.
그는 시험 결과를 기다리고 있다.

01 American
[əmérikən]

명 미국인 형 미국의
The American athlete won the race.
그 미국 운동선수가 그 경주에서 우승했다.

02 capital
[kǽpitəl]

명 수도
What is the capital of Russia?
러시아의 수도는 어디입니까?

03 Chinese
[tʃàiníːz]

명 중국인, 중국어 형 중국의
The site is also available in Chinese.
그 사이트는 중국어로도 이용할 수 있다.

04 citizen
[sítizən]

명 시민
This TV program is about a good citizen.
이 TV 프로그램은 한 선량한 시민에 대한 것이다.

05 city
[síti]

명 도시
The city has a long history.
그 도시는 오랜 역사를 가지고 있다.

06 connect
[kənékt]

동 연결하다, 연결되다
The two countries are connected by a canal.
그 두 나라는 운하로 연결되어 있다.

07 global
[glóubəl]

형 세계적인, 지구의
They will export these cars to the global market.
그들은 이 차를 세계 시장에 수출할 것이다.

08 Japanese
[dʒæ̀pəníːz]

명 일본인, 일본어 형 일본의
I became friends with the Japanese boy.
나는 그 일본 소년과 친구가 되었다.

09 Korean
[kərí(ː)ən]

명 한국인, 한국어 형 한국의
The foreigner can write his name in Korean.
그 외국인은 그의 이름을 한국어로 쓸 수 있다.

10 language
[lǽŋgwidʒ]

명 언어 ✿ native language 모국어
Her native language is English.
그녀의 모국어는 영어이다.

Daily Test

A 우리말 뜻과 일치하도록 빠진 글자를 써넣어 단어를 완성하세요.

1 연결하다, 연결되다 __ o __ n __ __ t

2 수도 __ __ p __ t __ __

3 세계적인, 지구의 __ __ __ b __ l

4 시민 __ __ t __ z __ __

5 미국인; 미국의 __ m __ __ __ c __ n

B 다음 영어 단어의 우리말 뜻을 쓰세요.

1 language _______________

2 Chinese _______________

3 city _______________

4 Japanese _______________

5 Korean _______________

C 우리말 뜻과 일치하도록 빈칸에 알맞은 단어를 써넣어 문장을 완성하세요.

1 The _______________ has a long history.
그 도시는 오랜 역사를 가지고 있다.

2 What is the _______________ of Russia?
러시아의 수도는 어디입니까?

3 This TV program is about a good _______________.
이 TV 프로그램은 한 선량한 시민에 대한 것이다.

4 The two countries are _______________ by a canal.
그 두 나라는 운하로 연결되어 있다.

5 The _______________ athlete won the race.
그 미국 운동선수가 그 경주에서 우승했다.

6 I became friends with the _______________ boy.
나는 그 일본 소년과 친구가 되었다.

7 The foreigner can write his name in _______________.
그 외국인은 그의 이름을 한국어로 쓸 수 있다.

8 The site is also available in _______________.
그 사이트는 중국어로도 이용할 수 있다.

11 leader
[líːdər]

명 지도자, 대표
As a leader, she attended the meeting.
대표로서, 그녀는 그 회의에 참석했다.

12 London
[lʌ́ndən]

명 런던
London is covered in thick fog now.
런던은 지금 짙은 안개에 덮여 있다.

13 New York
[nùːjɔ́ːrk]

명 뉴욕
Will you spend New Year's day in New York?
너희는 뉴욕에서 새해 첫 날을 보낼 거니?

14 Paris
[pǽris]

명 파리
The museum is located in Paris.
그 박물관은 파리에 위치해 있다.

15 peace
[piːs]

명 평화
They are doing their best to bring peace to the region.
그들은 그 지역에 평화를 가져오기 위해 최선을 다하고 있다.

16 Seoul
[sóul]

명 서울
I'm going to move to Seoul this weekend.
나는 이번 주말에 서울로 이사할 것이다.

17 society
[səsáiəti]

명 사회
Today's society has a lot of problems.
오늘날의 사회는 많은 문제를 가지고 있다.

18 trade
[treid]

명 거래, 무역
Trade between them will greatly increase.
그들 사이의 무역은 크게 증가할 것이다.

19 war
[wɔːr]

명 전쟁
The war continued for ten years.
그 전쟁은 10년 동안 계속됐다.

20 world
[wəːrld]

명 세계, 세상
Coffee is popular around the world.
커피는 세계적으로 인기가 있다.

Daily Test

A 우리말 뜻과 일치하도록 빠진 글자를 써넣어 단어를 완성하세요.

1 런던   _ o _ _ _ n   **2** 세계, 세상   _ _ r _ d

3 서울   _ _ _ u _   **4** 전쟁   _ a _

5 사회   _ _ c _ _ t _

B 다음 영어 단어의 우리말 뜻을 쓰세요.

1 Paris   _________   **2** leader   _________

3 trade   _________   **4** New York   _________

5 peace   _________

C 우리말 뜻과 일치하도록 빈칸에 알맞은 단어를 써넣어 문장을 완성하세요.

1 Today's __________ has a lot of problems.
오늘날의 사회는 많은 문제를 가지고 있다.

2 As a __________, she attended the meeting.
대표로서, 그녀는 그 회의에 참석했다.

3 I'm going to move to __________ this weekend.
나는 이번 주말에 서울로 이사할 것이다.

4 __________ between them will greatly increase.
그들 사이의 무역은 크게 증가할 것이다.

5 The museum is located in __________.
그 박물관은 파리에 위치해 있다.

6 The __________ continued for ten years.
그 전쟁은 10년 동안 계속됐다.

7 __________ is covered in thick fog now.
런던은 지금 짙은 안개에 덮여 있다.

8 Will you spend New Year's day in __________?
너희는 뉴욕에서 새해 첫 날을 보낼 거니?

 **Day 13** 상태

01 bright
[brait]

형 밝은
I love the large bright room.
나는 그 크고 밝은 방을 정말 좋아한다.

02 busy
[bízi]

형 바쁜
George is very busy with his homework.
George는 그의 숙제를 하느라 매우 바쁘다.

03 calm
[kɑ:m]

형 차분한, 평온한
The calm music makes you relax.
그 차분한 음악은 네가 긴장을 풀도록 해 준다.

04 certain
[sə́:rtən]

형 틀림없는, 확실한
It is certain that we will win the game.
우리가 그 경기에서 이길 것이 확실하다.

05 comfortable
[kʌ́mfərtəbl]

형 편안한
When does he feel most comfortable?
그는 언제 가장 편안함을 느끼니?

06 condition
[kəndíʃən]

명 상태
The old car is still in good condition.
그 오래된 차는 여전히 상태가 좋다.

07 convenient
[kənví:njənt]

형 편리한
A washing machine is really convenient.
세탁기는 정말 편리하다.

08 correct
[kərékt]

형 맞는, 옳은
The phone number is not correct.
그 전화번호는 맞지 않다.

09 dark
[dɑ:rk]

형 어두운
Walk carefully because it is pretty dark.
꽤 어두우니까 조심해서 걸어.

10 difficult
[dífəkʌ̀lt]

형 어려운
James solved the difficult problem in five minutes.
James는 그 어려운 문제를 5분 안에 풀었다.

A 우리말 뜻과 일치하도록 빠진 글자를 써넣어 단어를 완성하세요.

1 어려운   d _ _ _ _ c _ l _   2 차분한, 평온한   _ _ _ m

3 맞는, 옳은   _ o _ r _ _ _   4 틀림없는, 확실한   _ _ r _ a _ _

5 밝은   _ r _ _ _ t

B 다음 영어 단어의 우리말 뜻을 쓰세요.

1 comfortable   ________________   2 dark   ________________

3 condition   ________________   4 convenient   ________________

5 busy   ________________

C 우리말 뜻과 일치하도록 빈칸에 알맞은 단어를 써넣어 문장을 완성하세요.

1 I love the large ________________ room.
나는 그 크고 밝은 방을 정말 좋아한다.

2 It is ________________ that we will win the game.
우리가 그 경기에서 이길 것이 확실하다.

3 The ________________ music makes you relax.
그 차분한 음악은 네가 긴장을 풀도록 해 준다.

4 James solved the ________________ problem in five minutes.
James는 그 어려운 문제를 5분 안에 풀었다.

5 A washing machine is really ________________.
세탁기는 정말 편리하다.

6 The old car is still in good ________________.
그 오래된 차는 여전히 상태가 좋다.

7 George is very ________________ with his homework.
George는 그의 숙제를 하느라 매우 바쁘다.

8 Walk carefully because it is pretty ________________.
꽤 어두우니까 조심해서 걸어.

11　dirty
[də́:rti]

형 더러운
Let's sweep the dirty floor with a broom.
그 더러운 마루를 빗자루로 쓸자.

12　easy
[í:zi]

형 쉬운
It was easy to climb up the cliff.
그 절벽을 오르는 것은 쉬웠다.

13　equal
[í:kwəl]

형 동일한, 같은　동 같다
The soap and the dish are equal in price.
그 비누와 그 접시는 가격이 같다.

14　extreme
[ikstrí:m]

형 극도의, 극심한
He experienced the extreme cold.
그는 극도의 추위를 경험했다.

15　hungry
[hʌ́ŋgri]

형 배고픈
I gave some bread to the hungry cat.
나는 그 배고픈 고양이에게 빵을 좀 주었다.

16　necessary
[nésəsèri]

형 필요한
I'll bring all the necessary items in the lab.
나는 실험실에서 필요한 모든 물품들을 가져갈 것이다.

17　quick
[kwik]

형 빠른, 신속한
I'm expecting your quick reply.
나는 너의 빠른 답장을 기대하고 있다.

18　ready
[rédi]

형 준비가 된
Give me a call when you're ready.
너희가 준비가 되면 나에게 전화해.

19　thirsty
[θə́:rsti]

형 목이 마른
The thirsty man wanted a glass of water.
그 목마른 남자는 물 한 잔을 원했다.

20　wrong
[rɔ(ː)ŋ]

형 틀린, 잘못된
Your calculation is wrong.
너의 계산은 틀렸다.

Daily Test

A 우리말 뜻과 일치하도록 빠진 글자를 써넣어 단어를 완성하세요.

1 동일한, 같은; 같다 __ q __ __ __ __

2 목이 마른 __ __ __ r __ t __

3 더러운 __ i __ __ __

4 틀린, 잘못된 __ r __ __ g

5 극도의, 극심한 e __ t __ __ __ __

B 다음 영어 단어의 우리말 뜻을 쓰세요.

1 easy ________________

2 quick ________________

3 hungry ________________

4 ready ________________

5 necessary ________________

C 우리말 뜻과 일치하도록 빈칸에 알맞은 단어를 써넣어 문장을 완성하세요.

1 Your calculation is ________________.
너의 계산은 틀렸다.

2 Let's sweep the ________________ floor with a broom.
그 더러운 마루를 빗자루로 쓸자.

3 I'll bring all the ________________ items in the lab.
나는 실험실에서 필요한 모든 물품들을 가져갈 것이다.

4 It was ________________ to climb up the cliff.
그 절벽을 오르는 것은 쉬웠다.

5 Give me a call when you're ________________.
너희가 준비가 되면 나에게 전화해.

6 He experienced the ________________ cold.
그는 극도의 추위를 경험했다.

7 The ________________ man wanted a glass of water.
그 목마른 남자는 물 한 잔을 원했다.

8 I gave some bread to the ________________ cat.
나는 그 배고픈 고양이에게 빵을 좀 주었다.

01 accept [əksépt]
동 받아들이다
Are you going to accept her invitation?
너는 그녀의 초대를 받아들일 거니?

02 admit [ədmít]
동 인정하다
The boy has to admit his mistake.
그 소년은 그의 실수를 인정해야 한다.

03 believe [bilíːv]
동 믿다
They believe that she was a genius.
그들은 그녀가 천재였다고 믿는다.

04 consider [kənsídər]
동 고려하다, 여기다
They are considering adopting a child.
그들은 아이를 입양하는 것을 고려하고 있다.

05 forget [fərgét]
동 잊다　✿ forget-forgot-forgotten
Don't forget to check the list.
그 목록을 확인하는 것을 잊지 마.

06 guess [ges]
동 추측하다
You can guess what happened next.
너는 그 다음에 무슨 일이 일어났는지 추측할 수 있을 것이다.

07 hesitate [hézitèit]
동 망설이다
He didn't hesitate to apologize.
그는 사과하는 것을 망설이지 않았다.

08 idea [aidí(ː)ə]
명 발상, 생각
Sending flowers is a great idea.
꽃을 보내는 것은 아주 좋은 생각이다.

09 ignore [ignɔ́ːr]
동 무시하다
We must not ignore the good effects of TV.
우리는 TV의 좋은 효과를 무시해서는 안 된다.

10 image [ímidʒ]
명 이미지
He is a famous movie star with a clean image.
그는 깨끗한 이미지를 가진 유명한 영화배우이다.

Daily Test

A 우리말 뜻과 일치하도록 빠진 글자를 써넣어 단어를 완성하세요.

1 인정하다　　__ __ m __ __ __　　　　**2** 이미지　　__ __ __ g __

3 잊다　　__ __ __ g __ t　　　　**4** 믿다　　__ __ l __ e __ __

5 무시하다　　__ __ n __ r __

B 다음 영어 단어의 우리말 뜻을 쓰세요.

1 idea　　____________________　　**2** consider　　____________________

3 accept　　____________________　　**4** hesitate　　____________________

5 guess　　____________________

C 우리말 뜻과 일치하도록 빈칸에 알맞은 단어를 써넣어 문장을 완성하세요.

1 Are you going to ________________ her invitation?
너는 그녀의 초대를 받아들일 거니?

2 We must not ________________ the good effects of TV.
우리는 TV의 좋은 효과를 무시해서는 안 된다.

3 You can ________________ what happened next.
너는 그 다음에 무슨 일이 일어났는지 추측할 수 있을 것이다.

4 Don't ________________ to check the list.
그 목록을 확인하는 것을 잊지 마.

5 The boy has to ________________ his mistake.
그 소년은 그의 실수를 인정해야 한다.

6 He didn't ________________ to apologize.
그는 사과하는 것을 망설이지 않았다.

7 They are ________________ adopting a child.
그들은 아이를 입양하는 것을 고려하고 있다.

8 They ________________ that she was a genius.
그들은 그녀가 천재였다고 믿는다.

Day 14 생각과 인지

11 imagine
[imǽdʒin]

동 상상하다
Imagine that you meet a fairy.
네가 요정을 만난다고 상상해 봐.

12 intend
[inténd]

동 의도하다
I didn't intend to break the appointment.
나는 약속을 어길 의도는 아니었다.

13 judge
[dʒʌdʒ]

동 판단하다
We should not judge a person by appearance.
우리는 겉모습으로 사람을 판단하면 안 된다.

14 know
[nou]

동 알다, 알고 있다   ✿ know-knew-known
I know the secret of the treasure.
나는 그 보물의 비밀을 알고 있다.

15 knowledge
[nάlidʒ]

명 지식
He has a broad knowledge of the universe.
그는 우주에 관한 넓은 지식을 가지고 있다.

16 realize
[rí(:)əlàiz]

동 깨닫다, 알아차리다
The soldier realized the danger of his life.
그 군인은 그의 생명이 위험하다는 것을 깨달았다.

17 recognize
[rékəgnàiz]

동 알아보다, 인정하다
She didn't recognize the third man.
그녀는 세 번째 남자를 알아보지 못했다.

18 remember
[rimémbər]

동 기억하다
How can you remember all their names?
너는 어떻게 그들의 이름을 전부 기억하니?

19 thought
[θɔːt]

명 생각
The artist's thought was surprising at that time.
그 화가의 생각은 그 당시에는 놀라운 것이었다.

20 understand
[ʌndərstǽnd]

동 이해하다, 알아듣다   ✿ understand-understood-understood
I don't understand what you're saying.
나는 네가 하는 말을 이해하지 못하겠다.

A 우리말 뜻과 일치하도록 빠진 글자를 써넣어 단어를 완성하세요.

1 알다, 알고 있다   __ __ __ w   2 의도하다   __ n __ __ n __

3 생각   __ __ o __ __ __ t   4 판단하다   j __ __ g __

5 상상하다   __ __ a __ __ n __

B 다음 영어 단어의 우리말 뜻을 쓰세요.

1 recognize   __________   2 realize   __________

3 understand   __________   4 remember   __________

5 knowledge   __________

C 우리말 뜻과 일치하도록 빈칸에 알맞은 단어를 써넣어 문장을 완성하세요.

1 I didn't __________ to break the appointment.
나는 약속을 어길 의도는 아니었다.

2 We should not __________ a person by appearance.
우리는 겉모습으로 사람을 판단하면 안 된다.

3 __________ that you meet a fairy.
네가 요정을 만난다고 상상해 봐.

4 How can you __________ all their names?
너는 어떻게 그들의 이름을 전부 기억하니?

5 She didn't __________ the third man.
그녀는 세 번째 남자를 알아보지 못했다.

6 He has a broad __________ of the universe.
그는 우주에 관한 넓은 지식을 가지고 있다.

7 I __________ the secret of the treasure.
나는 그 보물의 비밀을 알고 있다.

8 I don't __________ what you're saying.
나는 네가 하는 말을 이해하지 못하겠다.

A 우리말 뜻에 해당하는 영어 단어를 찾아 동그라미 하세요.

| 런던 | 시작하다, 시작되다 | 거래, 무역 | 차분한, 평온한 | 알다, 알고 있다 |
| 인정하다 | 영향, 효과 | 도시 | 더러운 | 집중하다; 초점 |

b	g	j	c	a	l	m	b	a	j
z	e	f	f	e	c	t	h	d	s
f	f	g	x	k	n	o	w	m	t
w	o	h	i	s	g	c	t	i	t
j	s	c	b	n	d	i	r	t	y
v	q	h	u	c	b	t	a	y	z
n	t	c	z	s	n	y	d	h	p
L	o	n	d	o	n	f	e	c	g

B 우리말 뜻과 일치하도록 알맞은 단어를 골라 문장을 완성하세요.

| global | knowledge | image | case | effort | correct |

1 They will export these cars to the ________________ market.
그들은 이 차를 세계 시장에 수출할 것이다.

2 He is a famous movie star with a clean ________________.
그는 깨끗한 이미지를 가진 유명한 영화배우이다.

3 The doctor made an ________________ to cure her.
그 의사는 그녀를 치료하기 위해 노력했다.

4 He has a broad ________________ of the universe.
그는 우주에 관한 넓은 지식을 가지고 있다.

5 The phone number is not ________________.
그 전화번호는 맞지 않다.

6 In this ________________, ring the alarm bell first.
이런 경우에는, 먼저 비상벨을 울리세요.

Day 15_C

C 들려 주는 영어 단어를 바르게 쓴 다음, 우리말 뜻을 써넣으세요.

	영어 단어	우리말		영어 단어	우리말
1			11		
2			12		
3			13		
4			14		
5			15		
6			16		
7			17		
8			18		
9			19		
10			20		

D 우리말 뜻과 일치하도록 알맞은 단어를 골라 동그라미 하세요.

1 When does he feel most (comfortable / convenient)?
그는 언제 가장 편안함을 느끼니?

2 They are doing their best to bring (peace / capital) to the region.
그들은 그 지역에 평화를 가져오기 위해 최선을 다하고 있다.

3 My (goal / cause) is to renew my own record.
나의 목표는 나의 기록을 경신하는 것이다.

4 The soldier (understood / realized) the danger of his life.
그 군인은 그의 생명이 위험하다는 것을 깨달았다.

5 Her native (leader / language) is English.
그녀의 모국어는 영어이다.

6 I'm expecting your (quick / wrong) reply.
나는 너의 빠른 답장을 기대하고 있다.

E 영어는 우리말로, 우리말은 영어로 바꿔 쓰세요.

1	Chinese	____________	**2**	과정	____________
3	certain	____________	**4**	세계, 세상	____________
5	achieve	____________	**6**	의도하다	____________
7	ignore	____________	**8**	확인하다; 확인	____________
9	extreme	____________	**10**	뉴욕	____________
11	recognize	____________	**12**	어두운	____________
13	continue	____________	**14**	잊다	____________
15	hesitate	____________	**16**	끝내다, 끝나다; 끝	____________
17	wrong	____________	**18**	준비가 된	____________
19	society	____________	**20**	연결하다, 연결되다	____________

F 잘 듣고, 빈칸에 알맞은 단어를 써넣어 문장을 완성하세요.

Day 15_F

1 The foreigner can write his name in ________________.

2 I gave some bread to the ________________ cat.

3 The train was ________________ because of the heavy snow.

4 They are ________________ adopting a child.

5 I don't ________________ what you're saying.

6 The museum is located in ________________.

7 She ________________ him not to give up.

8 George is very ________________ with his homework.

Day 15

G 우리말 뜻과 일치하도록 빈칸에 알맞은 단어를 써넣어 문장을 완성하세요.

1 What is the c_________________ of Russia?
러시아의 수도는 어디입니까?

2 A washing machine is really c_________________.
세탁기는 정말 편리하다.

3 He c_________________ the report in a day.
그는 그 보고서를 하루 만에 완료했다.

4 The soap and the dish are e_________________ in price.
그 비누와 그 접시는 가격이 같다.

5 James solved the d_________________ problem in five minutes.
James는 그 어려운 문제를 5분 안에 풀었다.

6 H_________________ up, or we'll be late for the show.
서둘러, 그러지 않으면 우리는 그 쇼에 늦을 거야.

7 The artist's t_________________ was surprising at that time.
그 화가의 생각은 그 당시에는 놀라운 것이었다.

8 I'm going to move to S_________________ this weekend.
나는 이번 주말에 서울로 이사할 것이다.

9 I'm sure that you will s_________________.
나는 네가 성공할 것이라고 확신한다.

10 Are you going to a_________________ her invitation?
너는 그녀의 초대를 받아들일 거니?

✎ Review에서 틀린 문제의 영어 단어와 우리말 뜻을 쓴 다음, 영어 단어를 3번씩 쓰세요.

	( )	_________ _________ _________
	( )	_________ _________ _________
	( )	_________ _________ _________
	( )	_________ _________ _________
	( )	_________ _________

01	**attractive** [ətrǽktiv]	형 매력적인 The attractive singer has a lot of fans. 그 매력적인 가수는 팬이 많다.
02	**common** [kámən]	형 흔한, 평범한 Sam is a common English name. Sam은 흔한 영어 이름이다.
03	**crazy** [kréizi]	형 미친, 정상이 아닌 He is crazy to go there. 거기에 가다니 그는 정상이 아니다.
04	**diligent** [dílidʒənt]	형 성실한 The diligent student gets up at 6 a.m. 그 성실한 학생은 오전 6시에 일어난다.
05	**evil** [íːvəl]	형 사악한 In the movie, the hero beats the evil group. 그 영화에서, 그 영웅은 그 사악한 무리를 물리친다.
06	**famous** [féiməs]	형 유명한 ✿ famous for ~으로 유명한 The author is famous for her short stories. 그 작가는 그녀의 단편 소설로 유명하다.
07	**female** [fíːmèil]	형 여자인 명 여성 She is the first female mayor of Paris. 그녀는 파리의 첫 여성 시장이다.
08	**free** [friː]	형 자유로운 You are free to use the computer. 너는 그 컴퓨터를 자유롭게 써도 된다.
09	**great** [greit]	형 위대한 He is one of the world's greatest pianists. 그는 세계에서 가장 위대한 피아니스트 중 한 명이다.
10	**greedy** [gríːdi]	형 욕심 많은 I can't trust the greedy guy. 나는 그 욕심 많은 남자를 신뢰할 수 없다.

Daily Test

A 우리말 뜻과 일치하도록 빠진 글자를 써넣어 단어를 완성하세요.

1 자유로운   __ r __ __

2 흔한, 평범한   __ __ m __ __ n

3 미친, 정상이 아닌   __ __ __ z __

4 여자인; 여성   __ __ __ a __ e

5 사악한   e __ __ __

B 다음 영어 단어의 우리말 뜻을 쓰세요.

1 great   ________________

2 diligent   ________________

3 attractive   ________________

4 famous   ________________

5 greedy   ________________

C 우리말 뜻과 일치하도록 빈칸에 알맞은 단어를 써넣어 문장을 완성하세요.

1 The ________________ student gets up at 6 a.m.
그 성실한 학생은 오전 6시에 일어난다.

2 The author is ________________ for her short stories.
그 작가는 그녀의 단편 소설로 유명하다.

3 In the movie, the hero beats the ________________ group.
그 영화에서, 그 영웅은 그 사악한 무리를 물리친다.

4 He is ________________ to go there.
거기에 가다니 그는 정상이 아니다.

5 She is the first ________________ mayor of Paris.
그녀는 파리의 첫 여성 시장이다.

6 I can't trust the ________________ guy.
나는 그 욕심 많은 남자를 신뢰할 수 없다.

7 Sam is a ________________ English name.
Sam은 흔한 영어 이름이다.

8 The ________________ singer has a lot of fans.
그 매력적인 가수는 팬이 많다.

 **Day 16** 인물 묘사

11 intelligent
[intélidʒənt]

형 총명한, 똑똑한
The intelligent girl got a perfect score.
그 똑똑한 소녀는 만점을 받았다.

12 male
[meil]

형 남자의   명 남자
All the designers in the company are male.
그 회사에 있는 모든 디자이너들은 남자이다.

13 patient
[péiʃənt]

형 참을성 있는
The host is patient with the guests.
그 주인은 그 손님들에게 참을성 있게 대한다.

14 polite
[pəláit]

형 예의 바른, 공손한
His polite manner makes me comfortable.
그의 예의 바른 태도는 나를 편안하게 한다.

15 popular
[pápjələr]

형 인기 있는
My grandfather is a popular announcer.
나의 할아버지는 인기 있는 아나운서이시다.

16 responsible
[rispánsəbl]

형 책임감 있는
He is trying to be a responsible manager.
그는 책임감 있는 경영자가 되기 위해 노력하고 있다.

17 rude
[ru:d]

형 무례한
It is rude to point at a person.
사람을 손가락으로 가리키는 것은 무례하다.

18 strange
[streindʒ]

형 이상한
There is something strange about Arthur.
Arthur에게 이상한 점이 있다.

19 strong
[strɔ(:)ŋ]

형 강한, 힘이 센
Three strong men are carrying a piano.
힘이 센 남자 세 명이 피아노를 나르고 있다.

20 weak
[wi:k]

형 약한, 힘이 없는
The child is not weak anymore.
그 어린이는 더 이상 약하지 않다.

Daily Test

A 우리말 뜻과 일치하도록 빠진 글자를 써넣어 단어를 완성하세요.

1 예의 바른, 공손한 `_ _ l _ _ e` **2** 강한, 힘이 센 `_ t _ o _ _`

3 이상한 `s _ _ a _ _ _` **4** 남자의; 남자 `_ a _ _`

5 인기 있는 `_ _ _ u _ a _`

B 다음 영어 단어의 우리말 뜻을 쓰세요.

1 weak ___________________ **2** intelligent ___________________

3 patient ___________________ **4** rude ___________________

5 responsible ___________________

C 우리말 뜻과 일치하도록 빈칸에 알맞은 단어를 써넣어 문장을 완성하세요.

1 It is ________________ to point at a person.
사람을 손가락으로 가리키는 것은 무례하다.

2 He is trying to be a ________________ manager.
그는 책임감 있는 경영자가 되기 위해 노력하고 있다.

3 His ________________ manner makes me comfortable.
그의 예의 바른 태도는 나를 편안하게 한다.

4 Three ________________ men are carrying a piano.
힘이 센 남자 세 명이 피아노를 나르고 있다.

5 The host is ________________ with the guests.
그 주인은 그 손님들에게 참을성 있게 대한다.

6 The child is not ________________ anymore.
그 어린이는 더 이상 약하지 않다.

7 My grandfather is a ________________ announcer.
나의 할아버지는 인기 있는 아나운서이시다.

8 There is something ________________ about Arthur.
Arthur에게 이상한 점이 있다.

Day 17_01

01	**bottom** [bátəm]	몡 맨 아래, 바닥 The bottom of the stream consists of sand. 그 개울의 바닥은 모래로 이루어져 있다.
02	**center** [séntər]	몡 중심, 중앙 The bread has a hole in the center. 그 빵은 중앙에 구멍이 있다.
03	**close** [klous]	혱 가까운 뷔 가까이 The bank is close to the grocery store. 그 은행은 식료품 가게와 가깝다.
04	**direction** [dirékʃən]	몡 방향 Are we going in the right direction? 우리는 옳은 방향으로 가고 있나요?
05	**east** [iːst]	몡 동쪽 혱 동쪽에 있는 Which way is east? 어느 쪽이 동쪽이니?
06	**far** [fɑːr]	뷔 멀리 The post office is not far from here. 우체국은 여기에서 멀지 않다.
07	**front** [frʌnt]	몡 앞쪽 혱 앞쪽의 Did you lock the front door? 너는 앞문을 잠갔니?
08	**here** [hiər]	뷔 여기에서, 여기로 What are you doing here? 너는 여기에서 무엇을 하고 있니?
09	**inside** [insáid]	전 ~의 안에 뷔 안에 He allowed them to come inside. 그는 그들이 안에 들어오도록 허락했다.
10	**left** [left]	혱 왼쪽의 몡 왼쪽 Please raise your left hand. 당신의 왼손을 들어 주세요.

Daily Test

A 우리말 뜻과 일치하도록 빠진 글자를 써넣어 단어를 완성하세요.

1 가까운; 가까이   __ l __ __ e   **2** 여기에서, 여기로   __ __ r __

3 멀리   __ __ r   **4** 왼쪽의; 왼쪽   __ e __ __

5 앞쪽; 앞쪽의   __ r __ n __

B 다음 영어 단어의 우리말 뜻을 쓰세요.

1 east   _______________   **2** bottom   _______________

3 center   _______________   **4** inside   _______________

5 direction   _______________

C 우리말 뜻과 일치하도록 빈칸에 알맞은 단어를 써넣어 문장을 완성하세요.

1 The bread has a hole in the _______________.
그 빵은 중앙에 구멍이 있다.

2 What are you doing _______________?
너는 여기에서 무엇을 하고 있니?

3 Did you lock the _______________ door?
너는 앞문을 잠갔니?

4 The bank is _______________ to the grocery store.
그 은행은 식료품 가게와 가깝다.

5 He allowed them to come _______________.
그는 그들이 안에 들어오도록 허락했다.

6 Please raise your _______________ hand.
당신의 왼손을 들어 주세요.

7 Are we going in the right _______________?
우리는 옳은 방향으로 가고 있나요?

8 Which way is _______________?
어느 쪽이 동쪽이니?

11 near
[niər]

형 가까운　부 가까이
Where is the nearest parking lot?
가장 가까운 주차장은 어디에 있니?

12 north
[nɔːrθ]

명 북쪽　형 북쪽에 있는
The birds fly to the north in spring.
그 새들은 봄에 북쪽으로 날아간다.

13 opposite
[ápəzit]

형 맞은편의　전 ~의 맞은편에
We live on the opposite side of the hospital.
우리는 그 병원 맞은편에 산다.

14 outside
[àutsáid]

전 ~의 밖에　부 밖에
Let's take our dogs outside.
우리의 개들을 밖에 데리고 가자.

15 place
[pleis]

명 장소, 곳
Keep your passport in a safe place.
너의 여권을 안전한 장소에 보관해.

16 right
[rait]

형 오른쪽의　명 오른쪽
The man has a small scar on his right cheek.
그 남자는 그의 오른쪽 볼에 작은 흉터가 있다.

17 south
[sauθ]

명 남쪽　형 남쪽에 있는
The wind is blowing from the south.
바람이 남쪽에서 불어오고 있다.

18 there
[ðɛər]

부 거기에, 거기에서
My dad worked there as an engineer.
나의 아빠는 거기에서 엔지니어로 일하셨다.

19 top
[tɑp]

명 맨 위, 꼭대기　형 맨 위의
She was standing at the top of the stairs.
그녀는 계단 맨 위에 서 있었다.

20 west
[west]

명 서쪽　형 서쪽에 있는
Use the west entrance of the building.
그 건물의 서쪽 입구를 이용해.

Daily Test

A 우리말 뜻과 일치하도록 빠진 글자를 써넣어 단어를 완성하세요.

1 장소, 곳   __ l __ __ e   **2** 오른쪽의; 오른쪽   r __ g __ __

3 ~의 밖에; 밖에   __ __ __ s __ d __   **4** 가까운; 가까이   __ e __ __

5 서쪽; 서쪽에 있는   __ __ __ t

B 다음 영어 단어의 우리말 뜻을 쓰세요.

1 there   __________________   **2** south   __________________

3 north   __________________   **4** top   __________________

5 opposite   __________________

C 우리말 뜻과 일치하도록 빈칸에 알맞은 단어를 써넣어 문장을 완성하세요.

1 Use the __________________ entrance of the building.
그 건물의 서쪽 입구를 이용해.

2 The man has a small scar on his __________________ cheek.
그 남자는 그의 오른쪽 볼에 작은 흉터가 있다.

3 We live on the __________________ side of the hospital.
우리는 그 병원 맞은편에 산다.

4 The birds fly to the __________________ in spring.
그 새들은 봄에 북쪽으로 날아간다.

5 Keep your passport in a safe __________________.
너의 여권을 안전한 장소에 보관해.

6 My dad worked __________________ as an engineer.
나의 아빠는 거기에서 엔지니어로 일하셨다.

7 Let's take our dogs __________________.
우리의 개들을 밖에 데리고 가자.

8 The wind is blowing from the __________________.
바람이 남쪽에서 불어오고 있다.

Day 18 · 달력

01 January
[dʒǽnjuèri]

명 1월
The car sales increased in January.
자동차 판매량은 1월에 증가했다.

02 February
[fébruèri]

명 2월
You can buy the shelf in February.
너희는 2월에 그 선반을 살 수 있다.

03 March
[mɑːrtʃ]

명 3월
Ben closed his bakery last March.
Ben은 지난 3월에 그의 제과점을 닫았다.

04 April
[éiprəl]

명 4월
The band performs in the city every April.
그 밴드는 매년 4월에 그 도시에서 공연한다.

05 May
[mei]

명 5월
This tree will blossom in May.
이 나무는 5월에 꽃을 피울 것이다.

06 June
[dʒuːn]

명 6월
The waiter will start work from June 1.
그 웨이터는 6월 1일부터 일을 시작할 것이다.

07 calendar
[kǽləndər]

명 달력
The calendar contains beautiful photos.
그 달력에는 아름다운 사진들이 담겨 있다.

08 century
[séntʃəri]

명 100년, 세기
They moved to America in the 17th century.
그들은 17세기에 미국으로 이주했다.

09 month
[mʌnθ]

명 달, 월
She booked the restaurant a few months ago.
그녀는 몇 달 전에 그 식당을 예약했다.

10 year
[jiər]

명 해, 년
The kid is planning for next year.
그 아이는 내년 계획을 세우고 있다.

Daily Test

A 우리말 뜻과 일치하도록 빠진 글자를 써넣어 단어를 완성하세요.

1 달, 월   m _ _ _ _   **2** 3월   _ a _ _ h

3 6월   _ u _ _   **4** 100년, 세기   _ _ n t _ _ y

5 1월   _ _ _ u _ r _

B 다음 영어 단어의 우리말 뜻을 쓰세요.

1 May   **2** calendar

3 February   **4** April

5 year

C 우리말 뜻과 일치하도록 빈칸에 알맞은 단어를 써넣어 문장을 완성하세요.

1 The waiter will start work from ________________ 1.
그 웨이터는 6월 1일부터 일을 시작할 것이다.

2 This tree will blossom in ________________.
이 나무는 5월에 꽃을 피울 것이다.

3 The car sales increased in ________________.
자동차 판매량은 1월에 증가했다.

4 The kid is planning for next ________________.
그 아이는 내년 계획을 세우고 있다.

5 Ben closed his bakery last ________________.
Ben은 지난 3월에 그의 제과점을 닫았다.

6 They moved to America in the 17th ________________.
그들은 17세기에 미국으로 이주했다.

7 You can buy the shelf in ________________.
너희는 2월에 그 선반을 살 수 있다.

8 The ________________ contains beautiful photos.
그 달력에는 아름다운 사진들이 담겨 있다.

11 July
[dʒulái]

명 7월
She is expecting a baby in July.
그녀는 7월에 아기를 낳을 예정이다.

12 August
[ɔ́:gəst]

명 8월
We had a great vacation in August.
우리는 8월에 아주 멋진 휴가를 보냈다.

13 September
[septémbər]

명 9월
The film is released in September.
그 영화는 9월에 개봉된다.

14 October
[ɑktóubər]

명 10월
The tickets are available until October.
그 표들은 10월까지 사용할 수 있다.

15 November
[nouvémbər]

명 11월
My sister got married on November 11.
나의 누나는 11월 11일에 결혼했다.

16 December
[disémbər]

명 12월
Can you finish the job before December?
너는 12월 전에 그 일을 끝낼 수 있니?

17 Christmas
[krísməs]

명 크리스마스
The theater will be open on Christmas.
그 극장은 크리스마스에 문을 열 것이다.

18 Halloween
[hæ̀ləuí:n]

명 핼러윈
We made ghost costumes for Halloween.
우리는 핼러윈을 위해 유령 의상을 만들었다.

19 schedule
[skédʒu:l]

명 일정, 스케줄
I have a busy schedule on the weekend.
나는 주말에 일정이 바쁘다.

20 Thanksgiving
[θæ̀ŋksgíviŋ]

명 추수 감사절
They eat roast turkey on Thanksgiving.
그들은 추수 감사절에 구운 칠면조를 먹는다.

Daily Test

A 우리말 뜻과 일치하도록 빠진 글자를 써넣어 단어를 완성하세요.

1 7월   __ u __ __

2 10월   __ c __ __ __ __ r

3 일정, 스케줄   __ __ h __ __ u __ e

4 12월   __ __ c __ __ b __ __

5 핼러윈   __ __ l __ o __ __ e __

B 다음 영어 단어의 우리말 뜻을 쓰세요.

1 September   _______________

2 Thanksgiving   _______________

3 August   _______________

4 November   _______________

5 Christmas   _______________

C 우리말 뜻과 일치하도록 빈칸에 알맞은 단어를 써넣어 문장을 완성하세요.

1 The film is released in _______________.
그 영화는 9월에 개봉된다.

2 We had a great vacation in _______________.
우리는 8월에 아주 멋진 휴가를 보냈다.

3 We made ghost costumes for _______________.
우리는 핼러윈을 위해 유령 의상을 만들었다.

4 The theater will be open on _______________.
그 극장은 크리스마스에 문을 열 것이다.

5 Can you finish the job before _______________?
너는 12월 전에 그 일을 끝낼 수 있니?

6 She is expecting a baby in _______________.
그녀는 7월에 아기를 낳을 예정이다.

7 They eat roast turkey on _______________.
그들은 추수 감사절에 구운 칠면조를 먹는다.

8 My sister got married on _______________ 11.
나의 누나는 11월 11일에 결혼했다.

01 advise
[ədváiz]

동 충고하다

The coach advised her to get enough sleep.
그 코치는 그녀에게 충분히 잠을 자라고 충고했다.

02 against
[əgénst]

전 ~에 반대하여

All of them are against the war.
그들 모두는 그 전쟁에 반대한다.

03 argue
[á:rgju:]

동 논쟁하다, 주장하다

They are arguing about their travel route.
그들은 그들의 여행 경로에 대해 논쟁하고 있다.

04 choose
[tʃu:z]

동 선택하다, 고르다   ✿ choose-chose-chosen

We'll choose our baby's name from this list.
우리는 우리 아기의 이름을 이 목록에서 고를 것이다.

05 complain
[kəmpléin]

동 불평하다

She complained about the noise from outside.
그녀는 밖에서 들리는 소음에 대해 불평했다.

06 critical
[krítikəl]

형 비판적인

The critical article made her angry.
그 비판적인 기사는 그녀를 화나게 했다.

07 debate
[dibéit]

명 토론   동 토론하다

The debate was about the new medicine.
그 토론은 그 새로운 약에 관한 것이었다.

08 decide
[disáid]

동 결정하다

Why did he decide to cancel the picnic?
그는 왜 소풍을 취소하기로 결정했니?

09 decision
[disíʒən]

명 결정   ✿ make a decision 결정을 하다

They should make a quick decision.
그들은 신속한 결정을 해야 한다.

10 deny
[dinái]

동 부인하다, 부정하다

The police officer continued to deny the rumor.
그 경찰관은 그 소문을 계속 부정했다.

Daily Test

A 우리말 뜻과 일치하도록 빠진 글자를 써넣어 단어를 완성하세요.

1 충고하다   __ d __ i __ __

2 토론; 토론하다   __ e __ a __ __

3 비판적인   __ r __ __ i __ __ __

4 논쟁하다, 주장하다   __ r __ __ e

5 결정   d __ __ i __ __ __ __

B 다음 영어 단어의 우리말 뜻을 쓰세요.

1 against   _______________

2 deny   _______________

3 complain   _______________

4 decide   _______________

5 choose   _______________

C 우리말 뜻과 일치하도록 빈칸에 알맞은 단어를 써넣어 문장을 완성하세요.

1 The police officer continued to _______________ the rumor.
그 경찰관은 그 소문을 계속 부정했다.

2 All of them are _______________ the war.
그들 모두는 그 전쟁에 반대한다.

3 They should make a quick _______________.
그들은 신속한 결정을 해야 한다.

4 The coach _______________ her to get enough sleep.
그 코치는 그녀에게 충분히 잠을 자라고 충고했다.

5 Why did he _______________ to cancel the picnic?
그는 왜 소풍을 취소하기로 결정했니?

6 She _______________ about the noise from outside.
그녀는 밖에서 들리는 소음에 대해 불평했다.

7 We'll _______________ our baby's name from this list.
우리는 우리 아기의 이름을 이 목록에서 고를 것이다.

8 The _______________ article made her angry.
그 비판적인 기사는 그녀를 화나게 했다.

11 discuss
[diskʌ́s]

동 의논하다
Let's discuss the problem together.
그 문제를 함께 의논하자.

12 insist
[insíst]

동 주장하다
The boss insisted that everyone should come.
그 상사는 모든 사람이 와야 한다고 주장했다.

13 mean
[mi:n]

동 ~을 의미하다 ✿ mean-meant-meant
Do you know what I mean?
내 말이 무슨 의미인지 알겠어?

14 negative
[négətiv]

형 부정적인
She gave me a negative answer.
그녀는 나에게 부정적인 답을 주었다.

15 oppose
[əpóuz]

동 반대하다
Most students oppose the idea.
대부분의 학생들은 그 생각에 반대한다.

16 positive
[pázitiv]

형 긍정적인
Wendy is positive about her future.
Wendy는 그녀의 미래에 대해 긍정적이다.

17 recommend
[rèkəménd]

동 추천하다, 권하다
Can you recommend a good dentist?
좋은 치과 의사를 추천해 줄래?

18 request
[rikwést]

명 요청   동 요청하다
We accepted his request for an interview.
우리는 그의 인터뷰 요청을 받아들였다.

19 suggest
[səgdʒést]

동 제안하다
Mom suggested raising a pet.
엄마는 애완동물을 기르는 것을 제안하셨다.

20 true
[tru:]

형 사실인, 맞는
Unfortunately, the story is true.
유감스럽게도, 그 이야기는 사실이다.

Daily Test

A 우리말 뜻과 일치하도록 빠진 글자를 써넣어 단어를 완성하세요.

1 사실인, 맞는   __ __ u __   **2** 의논하다   __ __ s __ __ s __

3 반대하다   o __ p __ __ __   **4** 요청; 요청하다   __ e __ __ __ s __

5 부정적인   __ __ g __ t __ __ __

B 다음 영어 단어의 우리말 뜻을 쓰세요.

1 positive   _______________   **2** insist   _______________

3 suggest   _______________   **4** mean   _______________

5 recommend   _______________

C 우리말 뜻과 일치하도록 빈칸에 알맞은 단어를 써넣어 문장을 완성하세요.

1 Wendy is _______________ about her future.
Wendy는 그녀의 미래에 대해 긍정적이다.

2 Most students _______________ the idea.
대부분의 학생들은 그 생각에 반대한다.

3 Unfortunately, the story is _______________.
유감스럽게도, 그 이야기는 사실이다.

4 She gave me a _______________ answer.
그녀는 나에게 부정적인 답을 주었다.

5 Let's _______________ the problem together.
그 문제를 함께 의논하자.

6 Can you _______________ a good dentist?
좋은 치과 의사를 추천해 줄래?

7 Mom _______________ raising a pet.
엄마는 애완동물을 기르는 것을 제안하셨다.

8 We accepted his _______________ for an interview.
우리는 그의 인터뷰 요청을 받아들였다.

Review | Day 16~19

A 우리말 뜻에 해당하는 영어 단어를 찾아 동그라미 하세요.

충고하다	3월	여기에서, 여기로	무례한	약한, 힘이 없는
중심, 중앙	7월	남쪽; 남쪽에 있는	사실인, 맞는	미친, 정상이 아닌

c	f	h	s	d	c	r	a	z	y
e	v	n	e	w	j	t	n	J	x
n	a	M	a	r	c	h	p	u	w
t	d	d	h	m	e	g	b	l	t
e	v	t	r	u	e	r	t	y	f
r	i	l	j	t	s	o	u	t	h
j	s	z	x	b	m	v	s	d	j
w	e	a	k	w	s	d	x	c	e

B 우리말 뜻과 일치하도록 알맞은 단어를 골라 문장을 완성하세요.

arguing	greatest	free	bottom	April	far

1 The _________________ of the stream consists of sand.
그 개울의 바닥은 모래로 이루어져 있다.

2 They are _________________ about their travel route.
그들은 그들의 여행 경로에 대해 논쟁하고 있다.

3 You are _________________ to use the computer.
너는 그 컴퓨터를 자유롭게 써도 된다.

4 The band performs in the city every _________________.
그 밴드는 매년 4월에 그 도시에서 공연한다.

5 The post office is not _________________ from here.
우체국은 여기에서 멀지 않다.

6 He is one of the world's _________________ pianists.
그는 세계에서 가장 위대한 피아니스트 중 한 명이다.

Day 20_C

C 들려 주는 영어 단어를 바르게 쓴 다음, 우리말 뜻을 써넣으세요.

	영어 단어	우리말		영어 단어	우리말
1			11		
2			12		
3			13		
4			14		
5			15		
6			16		
7			17		
8			18		
9			19		
10			20		

D 우리말 뜻과 일치하도록 알맞은 단어를 골라 동그라미 하세요.

1 Use the (west / east) entrance of the building.
그 건물의 서쪽 입구를 이용해.

2 I have a busy (century / schedule) on the weekend.
나는 주말에 일정이 바쁘다.

3 The tickets are available until (October / December).
그 표들은 10월까지 사용할 수 있다.

4 Do you know what I (discuss / mean)?
내 말이 무슨 의미인지 알겠어?

5 The (patient / intelligent) girl got a perfect score.
그 똑똑한 소녀는 만점을 받았다.

6 The boss (insisted / decided) that everyone should come.
그 상사는 모든 사람이 와야 한다고 주장했다.

E 영어는 우리말로, 우리말은 영어로 바꿔 쓰세요.

1 month	___________	**2** 성실한	___________
3 responsible	___________	**4** ~의 밖에; 밖에	___________
5 deny	___________	**6** 1월	___________
7 east	___________	**8** 부정적인	___________
9 choose	___________	**10** 참을성 있는	___________
11 August	___________	**12** 달력	___________
13 famous	___________	**14** 결정하다	___________
15 Thanksgiving	___________	**16** 요청; 요청하다	___________
17 there	___________	**18** 강한, 힘이 센	___________
19 near	___________	**20** 12월	___________

Day 20_F

F 잘 듣고, 빈칸에 알맞은 단어를 써넣어 문장을 완성하세요.

1 The ________________ was about the new medicine.

2 The theater will be open on ________________.

3 The ________________ singer has a lot of fans.

4 The man has a small scar on his ________________ cheek.

5 Wendy is ________________ about her future.

6 You can buy the shelf in ________________.

7 All the designers in the company are ________________.

8 He allowed them to come ________________.

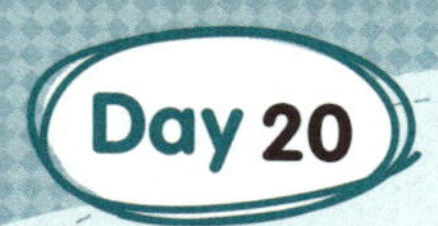

G 우리말 뜻과 일치하도록 빈칸에 알맞은 단어를 써넣어 문장을 완성하세요.

1 Please raise your l_________________ hand.
당신의 왼손을 들어 주세요.

2 My grandfather is a p_________________ announcer.
나의 할아버지는 인기 있는 아나운서이시다.

3 My sister got married on N_________________ 11.
나의 누나는 11월 11일에 결혼했다.

4 Can you r_________________ a good dentist?
좋은 치과 의사를 추천해 줄래?

5 We live on the o_________________ side of the hospital.
우리는 그 병원 맞은편에 산다.

6 She is the first f_________________ mayor of Paris.
그녀는 파리의 첫 여성 시장이다.

7 She c_________________ about the noise from outside.
그녀는 밖에서 들리는 소음에 대해 불평했다.

8 Are we going in the right d_________________?
우리는 옳은 방향으로 가고 있나요?

9 The waiter will start work from J_________________ 1.
그 웨이터는 6월 1일부터 일을 시작할 것이다.

10 Sam is a c_________________ English name.
Sam은 흔한 영어 이름이다.

Review에서 틀린 문제의 영어 단어와 우리말 뜻을 쓴 다음, 영어 단어를 3번씩 쓰세요.

01	**airplane** [ɛ́ərplèin]	몡 비행기 The airplane landed safely at the airport. 그 비행기는 공항에 안전하게 착륙했다.
02	**boat** [bout]	몡 (작은) 배, 보트 He is pulling the boat out of the water. 그는 그 보트를 물 밖으로 끌어 당기고 있다.
03	**crosswalk** [krɔ́(:)swɔ̀:k]	몡 횡단보도 Would you stop at that crosswalk? 저 횡단보도에서 멈춰 주시겠어요?
04	**fare** [fɛər]	몡 (교통) 요금 How much is the bus fare in London? 런던에서는 버스 요금이 얼마니?
05	**fasten** [fǽsən]	동 매다, 매이다 Please fasten your seat belts. 안전 벨트를 매 주세요.
06	**flight** [flait]	몡 비행, 항공편 The flight to Sydney will take ten hours. 시드니까지의 비행은 10시간이 걸릴 것이다.
07	**fuel** [fjú(:)əl]	몡 연료 She turned off the engine to save fuel. 그녀는 연료를 아끼기 위해 엔진을 껐다.
08	**helicopter** [héləkàptər]	몡 헬리콥터 The helicopter is flying above the lake. 그 헬리콥터는 호수 위를 날고 있다.
09	**highway** [háiwèi]	몡 고속도로 His car was broken down on the highway. 그의 차는 고속도로에서 고장이 났다.
10	**passenger** [pǽsəndʒər]	몡 승객 The passenger left his baggage on the bus. 그 승객은 그의 짐을 버스에 놓고 내렸다.

Daily Test

A 우리말 뜻과 일치하도록 빠진 글자를 써넣어 단어를 완성하세요.

1 (작은) 배, 보트　　　＿ ＿ ＿ t

2 비행, 항공편　　　＿ l ＿ ＿ h ＿

3 고속도로　　　＿ ＿ g ＿ w ＿ ＿

4 매다, 매이다　　　＿ ＿ s ＿ ＿ n

5 비행기　　　＿ i ＿ ＿ l ＿ n ＿

B 다음 영어 단어의 우리말 뜻을 쓰세요.

1 fare ＿＿＿＿＿＿＿＿＿

2 helicopter ＿＿＿＿＿＿＿＿＿

3 crosswalk ＿＿＿＿＿＿＿＿＿

4 passenger ＿＿＿＿＿＿＿＿＿

5 fuel ＿＿＿＿＿＿＿＿＿

C 우리말 뜻과 일치하도록 빈칸에 알맞은 단어를 써넣어 문장을 완성하세요.

1 Would you stop at that ＿＿＿＿＿＿＿＿＿?
저 횡단보도에서 멈춰 주시겠어요?

2 The ＿＿＿＿＿＿＿＿＿ to Sydney will take ten hours.
시드니까지의 비행은 10시간이 걸릴 것이다.

3 He is pulling the ＿＿＿＿＿＿＿＿＿ out of the water.
그는 그 보트를 물 밖으로 끌어 당기고 있다.

4 The ＿＿＿＿＿＿＿＿＿ is flying above the lake.
그 헬리콥터는 호수 위를 날고 있다.

5 The ＿＿＿＿＿＿＿＿＿ landed safely at the airport.
그 비행기는 공항에 안전하게 착륙했다.

6 Please ＿＿＿＿＿＿＿＿＿ your seat belts.
안전 벨트를 매 주세요.

7 How much is the bus ＿＿＿＿＿＿＿＿＿ in London?
런던에서는 버스 요금이 얼마니?

8 The ＿＿＿＿＿＿＿＿＿ left his baggage on the bus.
그 승객은 그의 짐을 버스에 놓고 내렸다.

11 **sail**
[seil]

동 항해하다   명 돛
They began sailing to India in May.
그들은 5월에 인도로 항해를 시작했다.

12 **ship**
[ʃip]

명 (큰) 배, 선박
The ship is entering the harbor slowly.
그 배는 천천히 항구로 들어오고 있다.

13 **station**
[stéiʃən]

명 역, 정류장
Get off at the next station.
다음 역에서 내려.

14 **subway**
[sʌ́bwèi]

명 지하철
The subway is crowded with people on Mondays.
지하철은 월요일에 사람들로 붐빈다.

15 **taxi**
[tǽksi]

명 택시
I caught a taxi near the bridge.
나는 다리 근처에서 택시를 잡았다.

16 **traffic light**
[trǽfiklàit]

명 신호등
A red traffic light means "Stop."
빨간색 신호등은 '멈추시오'라는 의미이다.

17 **train**
[trein]

명 기차, 열차
Can we check a train timetable on-line?
우리는 온라인으로 기차 시간표를 확인할 수 있니?

18 **truck**
[trʌk]

명 트럭
The truck will carry all the boxes to the town.
그 트럭은 그 모든 상자들을 그 도시까지 나를 것이다.

19 **vehicle**
[víːikl]

명 차량, 탈것
Which vehicle were you driving yesterday?
너는 어제 어느 차량을 운전하고 있었니?

20 **wheel**
[hwiːl]

명 바퀴
We had to change the front wheel.
우리는 앞바퀴를 바꿔야 했다.

Daily Test

A 우리말 뜻과 일치하도록 빠진 글자를 써넣어 단어를 완성하세요.

1 기차, 열차   __ r __ __ n   **2** 차량, 탈것   __ __ h __ c __ __

3 (큰) 배, 선박   __ __ __ p   **4** 택시   __ __ x __

5 트럭   t __ __ c __

B 다음 영어 단어의 우리말 뜻을 쓰세요.

1 station   __________________   **2** wheel   __________________

3 traffic light   __________________   **4** sail   __________________

5 subway   __________________

C 우리말 뜻과 일치하도록 빈칸에 알맞은 단어를 써넣어 문장을 완성하세요.

1 I caught a __________________ near the bridge.
나는 다리 근처에서 택시를 잡았다.

2 Can we check a __________________ timetable on-line?
우리는 온라인으로 기차 시간표를 확인할 수 있니?

3 A red __________________ means "Stop."
빨간색 신호등은 '멈추시오'라는 의미이다.

4 The __________________ is entering the harbor slowly.
그 배는 천천히 항구로 들어오고 있다.

5 We had to change the front __________________.
우리는 앞바퀴를 바꿔야 했다.

6 Get off at the next __________________.
다음 역에서 내려.

7 The __________________ will carry all the boxes to the town.
그 트럭은 그 모든 상자들을 그 도시까지 나를 것이다.

8 The __________________ is crowded with people on Mondays.
지하철은 월요일에 사람들로 붐빈다.

01 amazed
[əméizd]

형 놀란
The kids were amazed at a big shark.
그 아이들은 큰 상어를 보고 놀랐다.

02 anxious
[ǽŋkʃəs]

형 불안해하는
She was anxious about her election result.
그녀는 그녀의 선거 결과에 대해 불안해했다.

03 delight
[diláit]

명 기쁨
Meeting them is a great delight to me.
그들을 만나는 것은 나에게 큰 기쁨이다.

04 depressed
[diprést]

형 우울한
Simon is depressed by the bad weather.
Simon은 날씨가 안 좋아서 우울해한다.

05 emotion
[imóuʃən]

명 감정
He showed no emotion at the news.
그는 그 소식에 아무런 감정도 보이지 않았다.

06 excited
[iksáitid]

형 신이 난, 흥분한
Anna is excited to learn to surf this summer.
Anna는 이번 여름에 파도타기를 배우게 되어 신이 나 있다.

07 fantastic
[fæntǽstik]

형 환상적인
The adventure in the forest was fantastic!
숲 속에서의 모험은 환상적이었다!

08 funny
[fʌ́ni]

형 웃기는, 재미있는
Let me tell you a funny story about my childhood.
나의 어린 시절에 대해서 재미있는 이야기를 해 줄게.

09 happiness
[hǽpinis]

명 행복
Happiness is more important than money.
행복은 돈보다 더 중요하다.

10 horror
[hɔ́(:)rər]

명 공포
They couldn't move with horror.
그들은 공포로 움직일 수 없었다.

Daily Test

A 우리말 뜻과 일치하도록 빠진 글자를 써넣어 단어를 완성하세요.

1 웃기는, 재미있는   f __ __ n __

2 감정   __ m __ t __ __ __

3 공포   __ o __ r __ __

4 기쁨   __ __ l __ __ h __

5 신이 난, 흥분한   __ __ __ i __ __ d

B 다음 영어 단어의 우리말 뜻을 쓰세요.

1 happiness   _________________

2 amazed   _________________

3 depressed   _________________

4 fantastic   _________________

5 anxious   _________________

C 우리말 뜻과 일치하도록 빈칸에 알맞은 단어를 써넣어 문장을 완성하세요.

1 Simon is _________________ by the bad weather.
Simon은 날씨가 안 좋아서 우울해한다.

2 She was _________________ about her election result.
그녀는 그녀의 선거 결과에 대해 불안해했다.

3 They couldn't move with _________________.
그들은 공포로 움직일 수 없었다.

4 _________________ is more important than money.
행복은 돈보다 더 중요하다.

5 Meeting them is a great _________________ to me.
그들을 만나는 것은 나에게 큰 기쁨이다.

6 He showed no _________________ at the news.
그는 그 소식에 아무런 감정도 보이지 않았다.

7 The adventure in the forest was _________________!
숲 속에서의 모험은 환상적이었다!

8 Anna is _________________ to learn to surf this summer.
Anna는 이번 여름에 파도타기를 배우게 되어 신이 나 있다.

11 lonely
[lóunli]

형 외로운
She feels lonely especially in winter.
그녀는 특히 겨울에 외로움을 느낀다.

12 nervous
[nə́ːrvəs]

형 초조해하는
I'm always nervous before taking a test.
나는 항상 시험을 치기 전에 초조하다.

13 proud
[praud]

형 자랑스러워하는
We are very proud of our daughter.
우리는 우리의 딸이 매우 자랑스럽다.

14 scared
[skɛərd]

형 겁먹은, 무서워하는
The deer got scared and ran away.
그 사슴들은 겁을 먹고 도망갔다.

15 shy
[ʃai]

형 수줍음을 많이 타는
The shy girl is hiding behind her mom.
그 수줍음을 많이 타는 소녀는 그녀의 엄마 뒤에 숨어 있다.

16 sorrow
[sárou]

명 슬픔
My friend wanted to share my sorrow.
나의 친구는 나의 슬픔을 함께 나누고 싶어 했다.

17 surprised
[sərpráizd]

형 놀란
They were surprised at the new technology.
그들은 그 새로운 기술에 놀랐다.

18 upset
[ʌpsét]

동 속상하게 만들다   형 속상한   ✿ upset-upset-upset
He was upset because he lost his bag.
그는 그의 가방을 잃어버려서 속상했다.

19 wonder
[wʌ́ndər]

동 궁금해하다
She wonders who they are.
그녀는 그들이 누구인지 궁금해한다.

20 worried
[wə́ːrid]

형 걱정스러워하는
Your parents are worried about your safety.
너의 부모님은 너의 안전에 대해 걱정하신다.

Daily Test

A 우리말 뜻과 일치하도록 빠진 글자를 써넣어 단어를 완성하세요.

1 외로운   _ o _ _ l _   2 슬픔   _ _ r _ _ w

3 걱정스러워하는   w _ r _ _ _ d   4 궁금해하다   _ o _ _ e _

5 겁먹은, 무서워하는   _ c _ r _ _

B 다음 영어 단어의 우리말 뜻을 쓰세요.

1 shy   _______________   2 nervous   _______________

3 proud   _______________   4 surprised   _______________

5 upset   _______________

C 우리말 뜻과 일치하도록 빈칸에 알맞은 단어를 써넣어 문장을 완성하세요.

1 He was _______________ because he lost his bag.
그는 그의 가방을 잃어버려서 속상했다.

2 The _______________ girl is hiding behind her mom.
그 수줍음을 많이 타는 소녀는 그녀의 엄마 뒤에 숨어 있다.

3 We are very _______________ of our daughter.
우리는 우리의 딸이 매우 자랑스럽다.

4 She feels _______________ especially in winter.
그녀는 특히 겨울에 외로움을 느낀다.

5 Your parents are _______________ about your safety.
너의 부모님은 너의 안전에 대해 걱정하신다.

6 The deer got _______________ and ran away.
그 사슴들은 겁을 먹고 도망갔다.

7 I'm always _______________ before taking a test.
나는 항상 시험을 치기 전에 초조하다.

8 She _______________ who they are.
그녀는 그들이 누구인지 궁금해한다.

01　add
[æd]

동 추가하다, 덧붙이다
We have to add more sand to the soil.
우리는 그 흙에 모래를 더 추가해야 한다.

02　amount
[əmáunt]

명 양
They poured a large amount of water.
그들은 많은 양의 물을 부었다.

03　collect
[kəlékt]

동 모으다, 수집하다
He collects waste paper to recycle it.
그는 재활용하기 위해 폐지를 모은다.

04　create
[kriéit]

동 창조하다, 만들어 내다
Joe created a new radio program.
Joe는 새로운 라디오 프로그램을 만들었다.

05　decrease
[di:krí:s]

동 감소하다, 감소시키다
The number of orders decreased by 10%.
주문 수가 10% 감소했다.

06　develop
[divéləp]

동 개발하다
The company invested to develop a new machine.
그 회사는 새 기계를 개발하기 위해 투자했다.

07　factory
[fǽktəri]

명 공장
Debby works in a chocolate factory.
Debby는 초콜릿 공장에서 일한다.

08　handle
[hǽndl]

동 다루다
Do you know how to handle this system?
너는 이 시스템을 다루는 방법을 아니?

09　include
[inklú:d]

동 포함하다, 포함시키다
The price of the goods doesn't include tax.
그 상품의 가격은 세금을 포함하지 않는다.

10　increase
[inkrí:s]

동 증가하다, 증가시키다
The cost of building is expected to increase.
건축 비용이 증가할 것으로 예상된다.

Daily Test

A 우리말 뜻과 일치하도록 빠진 글자를 써넣어 단어를 완성하세요.

1 양   __ m __ __ n __

2 개발하다   __ __ v __ __ __ p

3 공장   __ __ __ t __ r __

4 다루다   __ __ n __ l __

5 추가하다, 덧붙이다   __ d __

B 다음 영어 단어의 우리말 뜻을 쓰세요.

1 increase   ___________________

2 create   ___________________

3 decrease   ___________________

4 include   ___________________

5 collect   ___________________

C 우리말 뜻과 일치하도록 빈칸에 알맞은 단어를 써넣어 문장을 완성하세요.

1 The company invested to _________________ a new machine.
그 회사는 새 기계를 개발하기 위해 투자했다.

2 We have to _________________ more sand to the soil.
우리는 그 흙에 모래를 더 추가해야 한다.

3 Debby works in a chocolate _________________.
Debby는 초콜릿 공장에서 일한다.

4 He _________________ waste paper to recycle it.
그는 재활용하기 위해 폐지를 모은다.

5 They poured a large _________________ of water.
그들은 많은 양의 물을 부었다.

6 The number of orders _________________ by 10%.
주문 수가 10% 감소했다.

7 The price of the goods doesn't _________________ tax.
그 상품의 가격은 세금을 포함하지 않는다.

8 Do you know how to _________________ this system?
너는 이 시스템을 다루는 방법을 아니?

11	**make** [meik]	통 만들다 ✿ make-made-made Is the T-shirt made of cotton? 그 티셔츠는 면으로 만들어졌니?
12	**prepare** [pripέər]	통 준비하다 She will prepare a list of her customers. 그녀는 그녀의 고객 목록을 준비할 것이다.
13	**produce** [prádʒuːs]	통 생산하다 We don't produce the microwaves anymore. 우리는 더 이상 그 전자레인지를 생산하지 않는다.
14	**product** [prádəkt]	명 생산물, 상품 They will release the new product tomorrow. 그들은 내일 그 새 상품을 공개할 것이다.
15	**provide** [prəváid]	통 제공하다 The hotel provides laundry service for guests. 그 호텔은 투숙객을 위해 세탁 서비스를 제공한다.
16	**reduce** [ridʒúːs]	통 줄이다 Let's talk about how to reduce pollution. 오염을 줄이는 방법에 대해 얘기해 보자.
17	**resource** [ríːsɔ̀ːrs]	명 자원 We must preserve natural resources. 우리는 천연자원을 보존해야 한다.
18	**sell** [sel]	통 팔다 ✿ sell-sold-sold The shop sells the guitars at high prices. 그 가게는 그 기타들을 높은 가격에 판다.
19	**sold out** [sòuldáut]	형 다 팔린, 매진된 The concert tickets are all sold out. 그 연주회 티켓은 모두 팔렸다.
20	**wrap** [ræp]	통 싸다, 포장하다 The present is wrapped in yellow paper. 그 선물은 노란색 종이로 싸여 있다.

Daily Test

A 우리말 뜻과 일치하도록 빠진 글자를 써넣어 단어를 완성하세요.

1 자원 r __ s __ u __ __ __

2 팔다 __ e __ __

3 생산하다 __ __ __ d __ c __

4 싸다, 포장하다 __ __ __ p

5 준비하다 __ r __ p __ __ __

B 다음 영어 단어의 우리말 뜻을 쓰세요.

1 product _________________

2 reduce _________________

3 sold out _________________

4 make _________________

5 provide _________________

C 우리말 뜻과 일치하도록 빈칸에 알맞은 단어를 써넣어 문장을 완성하세요.

1 Let's talk about how to _________________ pollution.
오염을 줄이는 방법에 대해 얘기해 보자.

2 The hotel _________________ laundry service for guests.
그 호텔은 투숙객을 위해 세탁 서비스를 제공한다.

3 The present is _________________ in yellow paper.
그 선물은 노란색 종이로 싸여 있다.

4 She will _________________ a list of her customers.
그녀는 그녀의 고객 목록을 준비할 것이다.

5 The shop _________________ the guitars at high prices.
그 가게는 그 기타들을 높은 가격에 판다.

6 They will release the new _________________ tomorrow.
그들은 내일 그 새 상품을 공개할 것이다.

7 We don't _________________ the microwaves anymore.
우리는 더 이상 그 전자레인지를 생산하지 않는다.

8 The concert tickets are all _________________ .
그 연주회 티켓은 모두 팔렸다.

01 address
[ǽdres]

명 주소
The mail was delivered to the wrong address.
그 우편물은 잘못된 주소로 배달되었다.

02 city hall
[sìtihɔ́ːl]

명 시청
Many people opposed building a new city hall.
많은 사람들이 새로운 시청을 짓는 것에 반대했다.

03 corner
[kɔ́ːrnər]

명 모서리, 모퉁이
I fell down at the corner yesterday.
나는 어제 모퉁이에서 넘어졌다.

04 curve
[kəːrv]

명 곡선, 커브
Please slow down at the curve.
커브에서는 속도를 줄이세요.

05 downtown
[dàuntáun]

부 시내에, 시내로
He opened a small bookstore downtown.
그는 시내에 작은 서점을 열었다.

06 fountain
[fáuntən]

명 분수
The fountain is in front of the theater.
그 분수는 극장 앞에 있다.

07 guide
[gaid]

명 안내, 안내인　동 길을 안내하다
We followed the tour guide into the old church.
우리는 관광 안내인을 따라 그 오래된 교회로 들어갔다.

08 landmark
[lǽndmàːrk]

명 주요 지형지물, 랜드마크
The Statue of Liberty is a well-known landmark.
자유의 여신상은 잘 알려진 랜드마크이다.

09 lead
[liːd]

동 이끌다, 연결되다　✿ lead-led-led
The path leads to the low hill.
그 길은 그 낮은 언덕으로 연결된다.

10 map
[mæp]

명 지도
We need a map to find an exact location.
우리는 정확한 위치를 찾기 위해 지도가 필요하다.

Daily Test

A 우리말 뜻과 일치하도록 빠진 글자를 써넣어 단어를 완성하세요.

1 지도   __ a __

2 모서리, 모퉁이   __ __ r __ e __

3 분수   __ o __ __ t __ i __

4 이끌다, 연결되다   __ e __ __

5 시내에, 시내로   __ __ w __ __ o __ __

B 다음 영어 단어의 우리말 뜻을 쓰세요.

1 city hall   _______________

2 address   _______________

3 curve   _______________

4 landmark   _______________

5 guide   _______________

C 우리말 뜻과 일치하도록 빈칸에 알맞은 단어를 써넣어 문장을 완성하세요.

1 He opened a small bookstore _______________.
그는 시내에 작은 서점을 열었다.

2 The path _______________ to the low hill.
그 길은 그 낮은 언덕으로 연결된다.

3 I fell down at the _______________ yesterday.
나는 어제 모퉁이에서 넘어졌다.

4 Please slow down at the _______________.
커브에서는 속도를 줄이세요.

5 The _______________ is in front of the theater.
그 분수는 극장 앞에 있다.

6 The mail was delivered to the wrong _______________.
그 우편물은 잘못된 주소로 배달되었다.

7 We need a _______________ to find an exact location.
우리는 정확한 위치를 찾기 위해 지도가 필요하다.

8 The Statue of Liberty is a well-known _______________.
자유의 여신상은 잘 알려진 랜드마크이다.

11	**neighbor** [néibər]	명 이웃 (사람) A new neighbor moved in last week. 새 이웃이 지난주에 이사를 왔다.
12	**neighborhood** [néibərhùd]	명 근처, 동네 This is a good neighborhood to raise children. 이곳은 아이들을 키우기에 좋은 동네이다.
13	**next-door** [nékstdɔ:r]	형 옆집의 He often complains about the next-door neighbor. 그는 종종 옆집 이웃에 대해 불평한다.
14	**point** [pɔint]	명 지점　동 가리키다 The man is pointing south. 그 남자는 남쪽을 가리키고 있다.
15	**road** [roud]	명 도로 The road repairs were completed yesterday. 도로 보수는 어제 완료되었다.
16	**show** [ʃou]	동 보여 주다, 알려 주다 Can you show me the way to the station? 역에 가는 길을 나에게 알려 줄래?
17	**street** [stri:t]	명 거리, 도로 The street was empty during the holidays. 그 거리는 휴일 동안 비어 있었다.
18	**town** [taun]	명 (소)도시, 시내 His family lives in this quiet town. 그의 가족은 이 조용한 도시에 산다.
19	**turn** [tə:rn]	동 돌다, 돌리다 Turn right at the bookstore and go straight. 서점에서 오른쪽으로 돌아서 곧장 가.
20	**village** [vílidʒ]	명 마을 What do you know about the village? 너는 그 마을에 대해 무엇을 알고 있니?

Daily Test

A 우리말 뜻과 일치하도록 빠진 글자를 써넣어 단어를 완성하세요.

1 지점; 가리키다 p __ i __ __

2 거리, 도로 __ __ r __ e __

3 (소)도시, 시내 __ __ w __

4 이웃 (사람) __ e __ __ h __ __ r

5 돌다, 돌리다 __ u __ __

B 다음 영어 단어의 우리말 뜻을 쓰세요.

1 neighborhood ________________

2 road ________________

3 village ________________

4 next-door ________________

5 show ________________

C 우리말 뜻과 일치하도록 빈칸에 알맞은 단어를 써넣어 문장을 완성하세요.

1 What do you know about the ________________?
너는 그 마을에 대해 무엇을 알고 있니?

2 The man is ________________ south.
그 남자는 남쪽을 가리키고 있다.

3 A new ________________ moved in last week.
새 이웃이 지난주에 이사를 왔다.

4 ________________ right at the bookstore and go straight.
서점에서 오른쪽으로 돌아서 곧장 가.

5 He often complains about the ________________ neighbor.
그는 종종 옆집 이웃에 대해 불평한다.

6 This is a good ________________ to raise children.
이곳은 아이들을 키우기에 좋은 동네이다.

7 His family lives in this quiet ________________.
그의 가족은 이 조용한 도시에 산다.

8 Can you ________________ me the way to the station?
역에 가는 길을 나에게 알려 줄래?

A 우리말 뜻에 해당하는 영어 단어를 찾아 동그라미 하세요.

공포	팔다	싸다, 포장하다	(작은) 배, 보트	자랑스러워하는
기차, 열차	다루다	(소)도시, 시내	이끌다, 연결되다	속상하게 만들다; 속상한

f	w	t	n	d	y	p	c	m	w
s	g	w	t	h	o	r	r	o	r
t	o	x	b	a	k	o	k	z	a
t	g	t	t	n	p	u	j	u	p
b	l	e	a	d	w	d	s	p	q
r	o	s	e	l	l	y	r	s	s
g	m	a	b	e	x	l	j	e	t
v	l	k	t	r	a	i	n	t	t

B 우리말 뜻과 일치하도록 알맞은 단어를 골라 문장을 완성하세요.

street	emotion	sailing	surprised	resources	collects

1 They began ________________ to India in May.
그들은 5월에 인도로 항해를 시작했다.

2 They were ________________ at the new technology.
그들은 그 새로운 기술에 놀랐다.

3 We must preserve natural ________________.
우리는 천연자원을 보존해야 한다.

4 He ________________ waste paper to recycle it.
그는 재활용하기 위해 폐지를 모은다.

5 He showed no ________________ at the news.
그는 그 소식에 아무런 감정도 보이지 않았다.

6 The ________________ was empty during the holidays.
그 거리는 휴일 동안 비어 있었다.

C 들려 주는 영어 단어를 바르게 쓴 다음, 우리말 뜻을 써넣으세요.

Day 25_C

	영어 단어	우리말		영어 단어	우리말
1			11		
2			12		
3			13		
4			14		
5			15		
6			16		
7			17		
8			18		
9			19		
10			20		

D 우리말 뜻과 일치하도록 알맞은 단어를 골라 동그라미 하세요.

1 Joe (created / included) a new radio program.
Joe는 새로운 라디오 프로그램을 만들었다.

2 He often complains about the (town / next-door) neighbor.
그는 종종 옆집 이웃에 대해 불평한다.

3 The kids were (excited / amazed) at a big shark.
그 아이들은 큰 상어를 보고 놀랐다.

4 Get off at the next (station / vehicle).
다음 역에서 내려.

5 We followed the tour (guide / address) into the old church.
우리는 관광 안내인을 따라 그 오래된 교회로 들어갔다.

6 She turned off the engine to save (fuel / sail).
그녀는 연료를 아끼기 위해 엔진을 껐다.

E 영어는 우리말로, 우리말은 영어로 바꿔 쓰세요.

1	anxious	2	트럭
3	include	4	외로운
5	corner	6	궁금해하다
7	crosswalk	8	지도
9	turn	10	분수
11	scared	12	비행, 항공편
13	neighborhood	14	준비하다
15	decrease	16	택시
17	sold out	18	신이 난, 흥분한
19	passenger	20	제공하다

F 잘 듣고, 빈칸에 알맞은 단어를 써넣어 문장을 완성하세요.

Day 25_F

1 They poured a large ________________ of water.

2 His car was broken down on the ______________.

3 The man is ______________ south.

4 Let me tell you a ______________ story about my childhood.

5 Please slow down at the ______________.

6 My friend wanted to share my ______________.

7 Is the T-shirt ______________ of cotton?

8 The ______________ is crowded with people on Mondays.

Day 25

G 우리말 뜻과 일치하도록 빈칸에 알맞은 단어를 써넣어 문장을 완성하세요.

1 The company invested to d________________ a new machine.
그 회사는 새 기계를 개발하기 위해 투자했다.

2 H________________ is more important than money.
행복은 돈보다 더 중요하다.

3 Many people opposed building a new c________________.
많은 사람들이 새로운 시청을 짓는 것에 반대했다.

4 Which v________________ were you driving yesterday?
너는 어제 어느 차량을 운전하고 있었니?

5 They will release the new p________________ tomorrow.
그들은 내일 그 새 상품을 공개할 것이다.

6 The a________________ landed safely at the airport.
그 비행기는 공항에 안전하게 착륙했다.

7 Simon is d________________ by the bad weather.
Simon은 날씨가 안 좋아서 우울해한다.

8 The r________________ repairs were completed yesterday.
도로 보수는 어제 완료되었다.

9 Please f________________ your seat belts.
안전 벨트를 매 주세요.

10 Your parents are w________________ about your safety.
너의 부모님은 너의 안전에 대해 걱정하신다.

Review에서 틀린 문제의 영어 단어와 우리말 뜻을 쓴 다음, 영어 단어를 3번씩 쓰세요.

01 a.m.
[èiém]
몡 오전
The museum opens at 9 a.m.
그 박물관은 오전 9시에 연다.

02 anniversary
[æ̀nəvə́:rsəri]
몡 기념일
Today is my parents' wedding anniversary.
오늘은 나의 부모님의 결혼기념일이다.

03 balloon
[bəlú:n]
몡 풍선
Ben decorated the dining room with balloons.
Ben은 식당을 풍선들로 꾸몄다.

04 celebrate
[séləbrèit]
통 기념하다, 축하하다
My relatives gathered to celebrate my graduation.
나의 친척들이 나의 졸업을 축하하기 위해 모였다.

05 ceremony
[sérəmòuni]
몡 의식, 식
He is hurrying to attend the awards ceremony.
그는 그 시상식에 참석하기 위해 서두르고 있다.

06 clock
[klɑk]
몡 시계
The clock on the wall struck twelve.
벽에 있는 시계가 12시를 쳤다.

07 congratulation
[kəngrætʃəléiʃən]
몡 축하 (인사)
She sent congratulations to the soccer team.
그녀는 그 축구팀에 축하 인사를 전했다.

08 costume
[kástʃuːm]
몡 의상
I wore a princess costume in the play.
나는 그 연극에서 공주 의상을 입었다.

09 event
[ivént]
몡 행사
Write down the place of the event.
그 행사의 장소를 적어 놔.

10 gift
[gift]
몡 선물
Dad is happy with the surprise gift.
아빠는 그 깜짝 선물에 행복해하신다.

Daily Test

A 우리말 뜻과 일치하도록 빠진 글자를 써넣어 단어를 완성하세요.

1 풍선   __ a __ l __ __ __ __   **2** 선물   __ __ f __

3 의식, 식   __ __ r __ m __ __ y   **4** 의상   __ __ s __ __ __ e

5 시계   c __ o __ __

B 다음 영어 단어의 우리말 뜻을 쓰세요.

1 anniversary   __________________   **2** a.m.   __________________

3 event   __________________   **4** celebrate   __________________

5 congratulation   __________________

C 우리말 뜻과 일치하도록 빈칸에 알맞은 단어를 써넣어 문장을 완성하세요.

1 The __________________ on the wall struck twelve.
벽에 있는 시계가 12시를 쳤다.

2 He is hurrying to attend the awards __________________.
그는 그 시상식에 참석하기 위해 서두르고 있다.

3 The museum opens at 9 __________________
그 박물관은 오전 9시에 연다.

4 My relatives gathered to __________________ my graduation.
나의 친척들이 나의 졸업을 축하하기 위해 모였다.

5 Ben decorated the dining room with __________________.
Ben은 식당을 풍선들로 꾸몄다.

6 Write down the place of the __________________.
그 행사의 장소를 적어 놔.

7 Today is my parents' wedding __________________.
오늘은 나의 부모님의 결혼기념일이다.

8 I wore a princess __________________ in the play.
나는 그 연극에서 공주 의상을 입었다.

11 hour
[auər]

圀 (시간 단위) 1시간
I'm going to meet them after an hour.
나는 한 시간 후에 그들을 만날 것이다.

12 invite
[inváit]

圀 초대하다
The lady invited her neighbors to dinner.
그 숙녀는 그녀의 이웃들을 저녁 식사에 초대했다.

13 minute
[mínit]

圀 (시간 단위) 분
The fireworks start in twenty minutes.
불꽃놀이는 20분 안에 시작한다.

14 o'clock
[əklák]

圀 ~시 (정각)
He will certainly be back before two o'clock.
그는 틀림없이 2시 전에 돌아올 것이다.

15 p.m.
[pìém]

圀 오후
The debate finished around 5 p.m.
그 토론은 오후 5시쯤에 끝났다.

16 parade
[pəréid]

圀 퍼레이드, 가두 행진
Where is the parade held?
그 퍼레이드는 어디에서 열리니?

17 party
[pá:rti]

圀 파티
I will bring some salad to the party.
나는 그 파티에 샐러드를 가져갈 것이다.

18 second
[sékənd]

圀 (시간 단위) 초
Wash your hands for ten seconds.
너의 손을 10초 동안 씻어.

19 time
[taim]

圀 시간, 때
She hates to waste time and money.
그녀는 시간과 돈을 낭비하는 것을 싫어한다.

20 watch
[wɑtʃ]

圀 손목시계
I forgot to set my watch.
나는 나의 손목시계를 맞추는 것을 잊었다.

Daily Test

A 우리말 뜻과 일치하도록 빠진 글자를 써넣어 단어를 완성하세요.

1 파티   __ a __ t __

2 시간, 때   __ __ m __

3 초대하다   __ __ v __ __ e

4 손목시계   w __ __ c __

5 (시간 단위) 분   __ __ n __ t __

B 다음 영어 단어의 우리말 뜻을 쓰세요.

1 o'clock   ______________

2 parade   ______________

3 hour   ______________

4 second   ______________

5 p.m.   ______________

C 우리말 뜻과 일치하도록 빈칸에 알맞은 단어를 써넣어 문장을 완성하세요.

1 I will bring some salad to the ______________.
나는 그 파티에 샐러드를 가져갈 것이다.

2 The fireworks start in twenty ______________.
불꽃놀이는 20분 안에 시작한다.

3 Where is the ______________ held?
그 퍼레이드는 어디에서 열리니?

4 Wash your hands for ten ______________.
너의 손을 10초 동안 씻어.

5 I'm going to meet them after an ______________.
나는 한 시간 후에 그들을 만날 것이다.

6 The lady ______________ her neighbors to dinner.
그 숙녀는 그녀의 이웃들을 저녁 식사에 초대했다.

7 I forgot to set my ______________.
나는 나의 손목시계를 맞추는 것을 잊었다.

8 The debate finished around 5 ______________
그 토론은 오후 5시쯤에 끝났다.

01 ability
[əbíləti]

명 능력

Jake has an ability to make people laugh.
Jake는 사람들을 웃게 만드는 능력이 있다.

02 challenge
[tʃǽlindʒ]

명 도전

I'm ready to accept the interesting challenge.
나는 그 재미있는 도전을 받아들일 준비가 되어 있다.

03 competitive
[kəmpétitiv]

형 경쟁을 하는, 경쟁력 있는

Our products are competitive in this market.
우리 제품들은 이 시장에서 경쟁력이 있다.

04 confidence
[kánfidəns]

명 자신감

She solved the problems with confidence.
그녀는 자신감 있게 그 문제들을 풀었다.

05 creative
[kriéitiv]

형 창조적인, 창의적인

The people were shocked by her creative design.
그 사람들은 그녀의 창조적인 디자인에 충격을 받았다.

06 excellent
[éksələnt]

형 훌륭한, 탁월한

Being an excellent actor requires much effort.
훌륭한 배우가 되는 것은 많은 노력을 요구한다.

07 expert
[ékspəːrt]

명 전문가

He is an expert on ancient art.
그는 고대 예술의 전문가이다.

08 genius
[dʒíːnjəs]

명 천재성, 천재

My little sister is a math genius.
나의 여동생은 수학 천재이다.

09 gifted
[gíftid]

형 (타고난) 재능이 있는

Picasso is one of the most gifted artists.
피카소는 가장 재능 있는 화가들 중의 한 명이다.

10 master
[mǽstər]

동 완전히 익히다, 숙달하다

Anna mastered various winter sports.
Anna는 다양한 겨울 스포츠를 완전히 익혔다.

Daily Test

A 우리말 뜻과 일치하도록 빠진 글자를 써넣어 단어를 완성하세요.

1 창조적인, 창의적인 __ __ e __ __ i v __　　**2** 능력 __ b __ l __ __ __ __

3 천재성, 천재 __ e __ __ u __　　**4** 도전 c __ a __ __ e __ __ __ __

5 전문가 __ __ p __ __ t

B 다음 영어 단어의 우리말 뜻을 쓰세요.

1 excellent __________________　　**2** master __________________

3 confidence __________________　　**4** gifted __________________

5 competitive __________________

C 우리말 뜻과 일치하도록 빈칸에 알맞은 단어를 써넣어 문장을 완성하세요.

1 She solved the problems with ________________.
그녀는 자신감 있게 그 문제들을 풀었다.

2 He is an ________________ on ancient art.
그는 고대 예술의 전문가이다.

3 The people were shocked by her ________________ design.
그 사람들은 그녀의 창조적인 디자인에 충격을 받았다.

4 Our products are ________________ in this market.
우리 제품들은 이 시장에서 경쟁력이 있다.

5 My little sister is a math ________________.
나의 여동생은 수학 천재이다.

6 Anna ________________ various winter sports.
Anna는 다양한 겨울 스포츠를 완전히 익혔다.

7 Picasso is one of the most ________________ artists.
피카소는 가장 재능 있는 화가들 중의 한 명이다.

8 I'm ready to accept the interesting ________________.
나는 그 재미있는 도전을 받아들일 준비가 되어 있다.

11 original
[ərídʒənəl]

형 독창적인
The students were inspired by his original ideas.
그 학생들은 그의 독창적인 생각들에 영감을 받았다.

12 perfect
[pə́ːrfikt]

형 완벽한
I think her performance was perfect.
나는 그녀의 공연이 완벽했다고 생각한다.

13 power
[páuər]

명 힘, 능력
You have the power to change yourself.
너는 자신을 변화시킬 힘을 가지고 있다.

14 professional
[prəféʃənl]

형 전문적인, 전문가의
The athlete needs professional help.
그 운동선수는 전문적인 도움이 필요하다.

15 skill
[skil]

명 기량, 기술
He learned the computer skills quickly.
그는 그 컴퓨터 기술들을 빠르게 배웠다.

16 special
[spéʃəl]

형 특별한
This is my grandma's special recipe.
이것은 나의 할머니의 특별한 요리법이다.

17 strength
[streŋkθ]

명 힘, 장점
What is your greatest strength?
너의 가장 큰 장점은 무엇이니?

18 talent
[tǽlənt]

명 재능
The kid had a great talent for singing.
그 아이는 노래에 대단한 재능이 있었다.

19 unique
[juːníːk]

형 유일무이한, 독특한
These paintings show his unique style.
이 그림들은 그만의 유일무이한 스타일을 보여 준다.

20 unusual
[ʌnjúːʒuəl]

형 특이한, 흔치 않은
I admire the scientist's unusual imagination.
나는 그 과학자의 흔치 않은 상상력을 존경한다.

Daily Test

A 우리말 뜻과 일치하도록 빠진 글자를 써넣어 단어를 완성하세요.

1 힘, 능력   __ __ w __ r

2 특별한   __ p __ __ i __ __

3 특이한, 흔치 않은   __ n __ s __ __ __

4 기량, 기술   __ __ i __ l

5 완벽한   __ __ __ f __ c __

B 다음 영어 단어의 우리말 뜻을 쓰세요.

1 talent   ________________

2 original   ________________

3 professional   ________________

4 unique   ________________

5 strength   ________________

C 우리말 뜻과 일치하도록 빈칸에 알맞은 단어를 써넣어 문장을 완성하세요.

1 You have the ________________ to change yourself.
너는 자신을 변화시킬 힘을 가지고 있다.

2 I think her performance was ________________.
나는 그녀의 공연이 완벽했다고 생각한다.

3 What is your greatest ________________?
너의 가장 큰 장점은 무엇이니?

4 The kid had a great ________________ for singing.
그 아이는 노래에 대단한 재능이 있었다.

5 These paintings show his ________________ style.
이 그림들은 그만의 유일무이한 스타일을 보여 준다.

6 The athlete needs ________________ help.
그 운동선수는 전문적인 도움이 필요하다.

7 The students were inspired by his ________________ ideas.
그 학생들은 그의 독창적인 생각들에 영감을 받았다.

8 This is my grandma's ________________ recipe.
이것은 나의 할머니의 특별한 요리법이다.

Day 28 — 대중문화

01 advertise [ǽdvərtàiz]
동 광고하다
We are making posters to advertise the product.
우리는 그 상품을 광고하기 위해 포스터를 만들고 있다.

02 article [ɑ́ːrtikl]
명 기사
She is collecting articles on global warming.
그녀는 지구 온난화에 관한 기사들을 모으고 있다.

03 audience [ɔ́ːdiəns]
명 청중, 관객
The audience clapped and cheered after the play.
관객들은 연극이 끝난 후에 박수를 치며 환호했다.

04 broadcast [brɔ́ːdkæst]
동 방송하다 명 방송 ✿ broadcast-broadcast-broadcast
The opening ceremony was broadcast on TV.
그 개회식은 TV로 방송되었다.

05 comic book [kámikbùk]
명 만화책
I spent the weekend reading comic books.
나는 만화책들을 읽으며 주말을 보냈다.

06 entertainment [èntərtéinmənt]
명 오락, 오락물
The show is family entertainment.
그 쇼는 가족 오락물이다.

07 fashion [fǽʃən]
명 유행, 인기, 패션
The actress was dressed in the latest fashion.
그 여배우는 최신 유행으로 옷을 입었다.

08 film [film]
명 영화, 필름
There is a big battle scene in the film.
그 영화에는 큰 전투 장면이 있다.

09 information [ìnfərméiʃən]
명 정보
The documentary offers useful information.
그 다큐멘터리는 유익한 정보를 제공한다.

10 interview [íntərvjùː]
동 인터뷰를 하다 명 인터뷰
Whom are you going to interview next?
너는 다음에 누구를 인터뷰할 거니?

Daily Test

A 우리말 뜻과 일치하도록 빠진 글자를 써넣어 단어를 완성하세요.

1 유행, 인기, 패션   f _ _ h _ _ _

2 청중, 관객   _ u _ i _ _ _ _ _

3 기사   _ r _ _ _ l _

4 영화, 필름   _ _ _ m

5 광고하다   _ d _ _ r _ _ s _

B 다음 영어 단어의 우리말 뜻을 쓰세요.

1 broadcast ________________

2 information ________________

3 entertainment ________________

4 interview ________________

5 comic book ________________

C 우리말 뜻과 일치하도록 빈칸에 알맞은 단어를 써넣어 문장을 완성하세요.

1 We are making posters to ________________ the product.
우리는 그 상품을 광고하기 위해 포스터를 만들고 있다.

2 The opening ceremony was ________________ on TV.
그 개회식은 TV로 방송되었다.

3 Whom are you going to ________________ next?
너는 다음에 누구를 인터뷰할 거니?

4 The documentary offers useful ________________.
그 다큐멘터리는 유익한 정보를 제공한다.

5 The ________________ clapped and cheered after the play.
관객들은 연극이 끝난 후에 박수를 치며 환호했다.

6 She is collecting ________________ on global warming.
그녀는 지구 온난화에 관한 기사들을 모으고 있다.

7 The actress was dressed in the latest ________________.
그 여배우는 최신 유행으로 옷을 입었다.

8 I spent the weekend reading ________________.
나는 만화책들을 읽으며 주말을 보냈다.

11 **magazine**
[mǽgəzìːn]

명 잡지
The magazine covers various topics.
그 잡지는 다양한 주제들을 다룬다.

12 **media**
[míːdiə]

명 대중 매체, 미디어
The media has a strong influence on teenagers.
대중 매체는 십 대들에게 강한 영향을 미친다.

13 **newspaper**
[njúːzpèipər]

명 신문
He usually reads a newspaper on the way to work.
그는 보통 출근길에 신문을 읽는다.

14 **perform**
[pərfɔ́ːrm]

동 수행하다, 공연하다
They perform abroad once a year.
그들은 일 년에 한 번 해외에서 공연한다.

15 **program**
[próugræm]

명 프로그램
What is the most popular program on TV?
TV에서 가장 인기 있는 프로그램이 무엇이니?

16 **public**
[pʌ́blik]

형 대중의 명 대중
The exhibition is open to the public.
그 전시회는 대중에게 공개된다.

17 **radio**
[réidiòu]

명 라디오
How often does she listen to the radio?
그녀는 라디오를 얼마나 자주 듣니?

18 **reporter**
[ripɔ́ːrtər]

명 기자, 리포터
The reporter wrote about the winner.
그 기자는 그 수상자에 대해 글을 썼다.

19 **speech**
[spiːtʃ]

명 연설
She gave a speech on the world economy.
그녀는 세계 경제에 대해 연설을 했다.

20 **television**
[téləvìʒən]

명 텔레비전
It's time to turn off the television.
텔레비전을 끌 시간이다.

Daily Test

A 우리말 뜻과 일치하도록 빠진 글자를 써넣어 단어를 완성하세요.

1 프로그램   __ r __ g __ __ m   2 연설   __ __ __ e __ h

3 대중 매체, 미디어   __ __ __ __ a   4 라디오   __ a __ __ o

5 잡지   m __ __ a __ i __ __

B 다음 영어 단어의 우리말 뜻을 쓰세요.

1 perform   _________________   2 reporter   _________________

3 television   _________________   4 public   _________________

5 newspaper   _________________

C 우리말 뜻과 일치하도록 빈칸에 알맞은 단어를 써넣어 문장을 완성하세요.

1 The _________________ covers various topics.
그 잡지는 다양한 주제들을 다룬다.

2 What is the most popular _________________ on TV?
TV에서 가장 인기 있는 프로그램이 무엇이니?

3 They _________________ abroad once a year.
그들은 일 년에 한 번 해외에서 공연한다.

4 How often does she listen to the _________________?
그녀는 라디오를 얼마나 자주 듣니?

5 He usually reads a _________________ on the way to work.
그는 보통 출근길에 신문을 읽는다.

6 The _________________ has a strong influence on teenagers.
대중 매체는 십 대들에게 강한 영향을 미친다.

7 The exhibition is open to the _________________.
그 전시회는 대중에게 공개된다.

8 The _________________ wrote about the winner.
그 기자는 그 수상자에 대해 글을 썼다.

01 ago
[əgóu]

(부) (얼마의 시간) 전에
The public library was established three years ago.
그 공공 도서관은 3년 전에 설립되었다.

02 already
[ɔːlrédi]

(부) 이미, 벌써
She already received the package.
그녀는 이미 그 소포를 받았다.

03 always
[ɔ́ːlweiz]

(부) 항상
Charles always keeps his room tidy.
Charles는 항상 그의 방을 깔끔하게 유지한다.

04 down
[daun]

(부) 아래로, 아래에
Please bend down and stretch your arms.
몸을 아래로 굽히고 팔을 뻗으세요.

05 hard
[hɑːrd]

(부) 열심히
My brother studies hard to become a lawyer.
나의 형은 변호사가 되기 위해 열심히 공부한다.

06 just
[dʒʌst]

(부) 꼭, 바로, 방금
This meat tastes just like chicken.
이 고기는 꼭 닭고기 같은 맛이 난다.

07 later
[léitər]

(부) 나중에, 후에
Two days later, they found the stolen car.
이틀 후에, 그들은 그 도난 당한 차를 발견했다.

08 much
[mʌtʃ]

(부) 매우, 많이
Don't worry too much about me.
나에 대해서 너무 많이 걱정하지 마.

09 never
[névər]

(부) 절대 ~ 않다
Tracy never eats fast food.
Tracy는 절대 패스트푸드를 먹지 않는다.

10 now
[nau]

(부) 지금, 이제
What is the most important problem now?
지금 가장 중요한 문제가 무엇이니?

Daily Test

A 우리말 뜻과 일치하도록 빠진 글자를 써넣어 단어를 완성하세요.

1 열심히   __ __ r __

2 꼭, 바로, 방금   __ __ __ t

3 항상   __ __ __ a __ s

4 지금, 이제   n __ __

5 (얼마의 시간) 전에   __ g __

B 다음 영어 단어의 우리말 뜻을 쓰세요.

1 already   ________________

2 much   ________________

3 never   ________________

4 down   ________________

5 later   ________________

C 우리말 뜻과 일치하도록 빈칸에 알맞은 단어를 써넣어 문장을 완성하세요.

1 What is the most important problem ________________?
지금 가장 중요한 문제가 무엇이니?

2 She ________________ received the package.
그녀는 이미 그 소포를 받았다.

3 Two days ________________, they found the stolen car.
이틀 후에, 그들은 그 도난 당한 차를 발견했다.

4 The public library was established three years ________________.
그 공공 도서관은 3년 전에 설립되었다.

5 My brother studies ________________ to become a lawyer.
나의 형은 변호사가 되기 위해 열심히 공부한다.

6 Charles ________________ keeps his room tidy.
Charles는 항상 그의 방을 깔끔하게 유지한다.

7 Tracy ________________ eats fast food.
Tracy는 절대 패스트푸드를 먹지 않는다.

8 Don't worry too ________________ about me.
나에 대해서 너무 많이 걱정하지 마.

11 often [ɔ́(:)fən]
- 부 자주, 종종

My daughter and I often go to the park.
나의 딸과 나는 자주 공원에 간다.

12 only [óunli]
- 부 오직, ~만

Only three people raised their hands.
오직 세 명의 사람들만 손을 들었다.

13 sometimes [sʌ́mtàimz]
- 부 때때로, 가끔

The firefighter sometimes saves injured animals.
그 소방관은 때때로 다친 동물들을 구조한다.

14 soon [su:n]
- 부 곧, 머지않아

We hope she will be better soon.
우리는 그녀가 곧 좋아지기를 바란다.

15 still [stil]
- 부 아직(도), 여전히

Are you still afraid of sleeping alone?
너는 아직도 혼자 자는 것을 무서워하니?

16 then [ðen]
- 부 그때

Everyone heard a loud noise then.
모든 사람이 그때 큰 소리를 들었다.

17 up [ʌp]
- 부 위로, 위에

An airplane is up in the sky.
비행기 한 대가 하늘 위에 있다.

18 usually [júːʒuəli]
- 부 보통, 대개

He usually wears a T-shirt and jeans to work.
그는 보통 티셔츠와 청바지를 입고 회사에 간다.

19 very [véri]
- 부 매우, 아주, 정말

The cliff is very high and steep.
그 절벽은 매우 높고 가파르다.

20 well [wel]
- 부 잘, 좋게

Add some sugar to the flour and mix well.
그 밀가루에 설탕을 조금 넣고 잘 섞어.

Daily Test

A 우리말 뜻과 일치하도록 빠진 글자를 써넣어 단어를 완성하세요.

1 곧, 머지않아   __ o __ __

2 그때   __ __ __ n

3 오직, ~만   __ __ l __

4 자주, 종종   __ f __ e __

5 아직(도), 여전히   s __ i __ __

B 다음 영어 단어의 우리말 뜻을 쓰세요.

1 up   _______________

2 usually   _______________

3 sometimes   _______________

4 well   _______________

5 very   _______________

C 우리말 뜻과 일치하도록 빈칸에 알맞은 단어를 써넣어 문장을 완성하세요.

1 The firefighter _______________ saves injured animals.
그 소방관은 때때로 다친 동물들을 구조한다.

2 _______________ three people raised their hands.
오직 세 명의 사람들만 손을 들었다.

3 He _______________ wears a T-shirt and jeans to work.
그는 보통 티셔츠와 청바지를 입고 회사에 간다.

4 An airplane is _______________ in the sky.
비행기 한 대가 하늘 위에 있다.

5 My daughter and I _______________ go to the park.
나의 딸과 나는 자주 공원에 간다.

6 Are you _______________ afraid of sleeping alone?
너는 아직도 혼자 자는 것을 무서워하니?

7 Add some sugar to the flour and mix _______________.
그 밀가루에 설탕을 조금 넣고 잘 섞어.

8 We hope she will be better _______________.
우리는 그녀가 곧 좋아지기를 바란다.

A 우리말 뜻에 해당하는 영어 단어를 찾아 동그라미 하세요.

자주, 종종	힘, 능력	재능	매우, 많이	유행, 인기, 패션
라디오	열심히	행사	손목시계	(타고난) 재능이 있는

o	l	t	a	l	e	n	t	b	g
f	w	k	x	w	t	b	j	k	i
t	f	q	c	a	d	b	h	l	f
e	v	e	n	t	r	g	a	c	t
n	t	n	d	c	f	a	r	m	e
s	m	u	c	h	r	r	d	l	d
y	n	p	o	w	e	r	j	i	p
f	a	s	h	i	o	n	p	r	o

B 우리말 뜻과 일치하도록 알맞은 단어를 골라 문장을 완성하세요.

ability   down   anniversary   comic books   speech   o'clock

1 Today is my parents' wedding ________________.
오늘은 나의 부모님의 결혼기념일이다.

2 Jake has an ________________ to make people laugh.
Jake는 사람들을 웃게 만드는 능력이 있다.

3 She gave a ________________ on the world economy.
그녀는 세계 경제에 대해 연설을 했다.

4 He will certainly be back before two ________________.
그는 틀림없이 2시 전에 돌아올 것이다.

5 Please bend ________________ and stretch your arms.
몸을 아래로 굽히고 팔을 뻗으세요.

6 I spent the weekend reading ________________.
나는 만화책들을 읽으며 주말을 보냈다.

Day 30

C 들려 주는 영어 단어를 바르게 쓴 다음, 우리말 뜻을 써넣으세요.

Day 30_C

	영어 단어	우리말		영어 단어	우리말
1			11		
2			12		
3			13		
4			14		
5			15		
6			16		
7			17		
8			18		
9			19		
10			20		

D 우리말 뜻과 일치하도록 알맞은 단어를 골라 동그라미 하세요.

1 There is a big battle scene in the (film / article).
그 영화에는 큰 전투 장면이 있다.

2 She hates to waste (hour / time) and money.
그녀는 시간과 돈을 낭비하는 것을 싫어한다.

3 Being an (excellent / original) actor requires much effort.
훌륭한 배우가 되는 것은 많은 노력을 요구한다.

4 Everyone heard a loud noise (then / soon).
모든 사람이 그때 큰 소리를 들었다.

5 This meat tastes (just / very) like chicken.
이 고기는 꼭 닭고기 같은 맛이 난다.

6 He learned the computer (strengths / skills) quickly.
그는 그 컴퓨터 기술들을 빠르게 배웠다.

 영어는 우리말로, 우리말은 영어로 바꿔 쓰세요.

1	creative	2	초대하다
3	a.m.	4	정보
5	ago	6	오직, ~만
7	usually	8	시계
9	special	10	독창적인
11	audience	12	광고하다
13	soon	14	파티
15	challenge	16	신문
17	program	18	선물
19	unique	20	나중에, 후에

Day 30_F

 잘 듣고, 빈칸에 알맞은 단어를 써넣어 문장을 완성하세요.

1 She sent _______________ to the soccer team.

2 I think her performance was _______________.

3 What is the most important problem _______________?

4 Whom are you going to _______________ next?

5 The debate finished around 5 _______________

6 An airplane is _______________ in the sky.

7 It's time to turn off the _______________.

8 He is an _______________ on ancient art.

G 우리말 뜻과 일치하도록 빈칸에 알맞은 단어를 써넣어 문장을 완성하세요.

1 The show is family e_________________.
그 쇼는 가족 오락물이다.

2 Ben decorated the dining room with b_______________.
Ben은 식당을 풍선들로 꾸몄다.

3 Our products are c_________________ in this market.
우리 제품들은 이 시장에서 경쟁력이 있다.

4 The cliff is v_________________ high and steep.
그 절벽은 매우 높고 가파르다.

5 The m_________________ has a strong influence on teenagers.
대중 매체는 십 대들에게 강한 영향을 미친다.

6 My relatives gathered to c_________________ my graduation.
나의 친척들이 나의 졸업을 축하하기 위해 모였다.

7 She a_________________ received the package.
그녀는 이미 그 소포를 받았다.

8 The exhibition is open to the p_________________.
그 전시회는 대중에게 공개된다.

9 I admire the scientist's u_________________ imagination.
나는 그 과학자의 흔치 않은 상상력을 존경한다.

10 Where is the p_________________ held?
그 퍼레이드는 어디에서 열리니?

Review에서 틀린 문제의 영어 단어와 우리말 뜻을 쓴 다음, 영어 단어를 3번씩 쓰세요.

	( )	______________ ______________ ______________
	( )	______________ ______________ ______________
	( )	______________ ______________ ______________
	( )	______________ ______________ ______________
	( )	______________ ______________ ______________

Phonics Check

Day 31~35

모르는 단어라서 읽을 수 없다고요?
Phonics를 알면 어떤 단어도 읽을 수 있어요.
Phonics 점검을 통해 영어 자신감을 길러요.

Check! R-controlled vowels를 익혀서
단어를 원어민처럼 읽어 보세요.

 **Day 31**   **-ar-**

01	**arm** [ɑːrm]	명 팔 She lifted her arms straight up. 그녀는 그녀의 팔을 위로 쭉 뻗었다.
02	**bar** [bɑːr]	명 막대, 바 Mom allowed me to buy a bar of chocolate. 엄마는 내가 초콜릿 바 한 개를 사는 것을 허락하셨다.
03	**bark** [bɑːrk]	동 (개가) 짖다 The neighbor's dog sometimes barks at night. 이웃의 개는 때때로 밤에 짖는다.
04	**barn** [bɑːrn]	명 헛간, 외양간 The boy is sitting in the corner of the barn. 그 소년은 헛간의 구석에 앉아 있다.
05	**card** [kɑːrd]	명 카드 Did you send the invitation cards to your classmates? 너는 너의 반 친구들에게 초대장을 보냈니?
06	**farm** [fɑːrm]	명 농장 We grow many vegetables on our farm. 우리는 우리의 농장에서 많은 채소를 키운다.
07	**guitar** [gitɑ́ːr]	명 기타 A guitar is a musical instrument with six strings. 기타는 여섯 개의 줄을 가진 악기이다.
08	**hard** [hɑːrd]	형 단단한 부 열심히 The hard box is not broken easily. 그 단단한 상자는 쉽게 깨지지 않는다.
09	**harm** [hɑːrm]	명 해, 피해 동 해치다 ✿ do harm 해를 끼치다 Some factories do harm to the environment. 어떤 공장들은 환경에 해를 끼친다.
10	**jar** [dʒɑːr]	명 병, 단지 The glass jars are displayed on the shelf. 그 유리병들은 선반 위에 전시되어 있다.

Daily Test

A 우리말 뜻과 일치하도록 빠진 글자를 써넣어 단어를 완성하세요.

1 농장   __ a __ __

2 (개가) 짖다   __ __ __ k

3 카드   c __ __ __

4 해, 피해; 해치다   __ __ r __

5 기타   __ __ i __ a __

B 다음 영어 단어의 우리말 뜻을 쓰세요.

1 arm   _________________

2 jar   _________________

3 barn   _________________

4 hard   _________________

5 bar   _________________

C 우리말 뜻과 일치하도록 빈칸에 알맞은 단어를 써넣어 문장을 완성하세요.

1 A _________________ is a musical instrument with six strings.
기타는 여섯 개의 줄을 가진 악기이다.

2 We grow many vegetables on our _________________.
우리는 우리의 농장에서 많은 채소를 키운다.

3 The neighbor's dog sometimes _________________ at night.
이웃의 개는 때때로 밤에 짖는다.

4 The _________________ box is not broken easily.
그 단단한 상자는 쉽게 깨지지 않는다.

5 Some factories do _________________ to the environment.
어떤 공장들은 환경에 해를 끼친다.

6 Mom allowed me to buy a _________________ of chocolate.
엄마는 내가 초콜릿 바 한 개를 사는 것을 허락하셨다.

7 The boy is sitting in the corner of the _________________.
그 소년은 헛간의 구석에 앉아 있다.

8 The glass _________________ are displayed on the shelf.
그 유리병들은 선반 위에 전시되어 있다.

Day 31 -ar-

11 March
[mɑːrtʃ]
명 3월
The magazine will be published next March.
그 잡지는 내년 3월에 발행될 것이다.

12 park
[pɑːrk]
명 공원 동 주차하다
You should not park your car here.
너는 여기에 너의 차를 주차하지 않는 것이 좋겠다.

13 part
[pɑːrt]
명 일부, 부분
This part of your brain controls emotions.
너의 뇌에서 이 부분이 감정을 조절한다.

14 party
[páːrti]
명 파티 ✿ throw a party 파티를 열다
She threw a small party for her husband.
그녀는 그녀의 남편을 위해서 작은 파티를 열었다.

15 scar
[skɑːr]
명 흉터
The woman wants to hide the scar.
그 여자는 그 흉터를 가리고 싶어 한다.

16 sharp
[ʃɑːrp]
형 날카로운, 뾰족한
The crocodile's teeth are so sharp.
그 악어의 이빨은 매우 날카롭다.

17 smart
[smɑːrt]
형 똑똑한, 영리한
The lawyer is smart and friendly.
그 변호사는 똑똑하고 친절하다.

18 star
[stɑːr]
명 별, 별 모양
Julia is observing stars with a telescope.
Julia는 망원경으로 별들을 관찰하고 있다.

19 start
[stɑːrt]
동 시작하다 명 시작
My uncle will start a business next month.
나의 삼촌은 다음 달에 사업을 시작할 것이다.

20 yard
[jɑːrd]
명 마당, 뜰
Can you rake the fallen leaves in the yard?
마당에 있는 낙엽들을 갈퀴로 모아 줄래?

Daily Test

A 우리말 뜻과 일치하도록 빠진 글자를 써넣어 단어를 완성하세요.

1 흉터   __ c __ __

2 시작하다; 시작   __ __ a __ t

3 일부, 부분   __ __ r __

4 별, 별 모양   s __ __ __

5 똑똑한, 영리한   __ m __ r __

B 다음 영어 단어의 우리말 뜻을 쓰세요.

1 March   ________________

2 yard   ________________

3 park   ________________

4 sharp   ________________

5 party   ________________

C 우리말 뜻과 일치하도록 빈칸에 알맞은 단어를 써넣어 문장을 완성하세요.

1 The magazine will be published next ________________.
그 잡지는 내년 3월에 발행될 것이다.

2 You should not ________________ your car here.
너는 여기에 너의 차를 주차하지 않는 것이 좋겠다.

3 She threw a small ________________ for her husband.
그녀는 그녀의 남편을 위해서 작은 파티를 열었다.

4 My uncle will ________________ a business next month.
나의 삼촌은 다음 달에 사업을 시작할 것이다.

5 Julia is observing ________________ with a telescope.
Julia는 망원경으로 별들을 관찰하고 있다.

6 The crocodile's teeth are so ________________.
그 악어의 이빨은 매우 날카롭다.

7 This ________________ of your brain controls emotions.
너의 뇌에서 이 부분이 감정을 조절한다.

8 The woman wants to hide the ________________.
그 여자는 그 흉터를 가리고 싶어 한다.

Day 32 -er

01 after [ǽftər]
전 접 ~ 뒤에, ~ 후에
I closed the door after they went outside.
그들이 밖으로 나간 뒤에 나는 문을 닫았다.

02 butter [bʌ́tər]
명 버터
The butter is melting on the hot bread.
그 버터가 뜨거운 빵 위에서 녹고 있다.

03 daughter [dɔ́:tər]
명 딸
My daughter likes horror movies.
나의 딸은 공포 영화를 좋아한다.

04 driver [dráivər]
명 운전자, 기사
The bus driver drives slowly around the school.
그 버스 기사는 학교 주위에서 천천히 운전한다.

05 eraser [iréisər]
명 지우개
Whose is the eraser in the drawer?
서랍 안에 있는 지우개는 누구의 것이니?

06 flower [fláuər]
명 꽃
She put the pink flowers in the vase.
그녀는 그 분홍색 꽃들을 꽃병에 꽂았다.

07 ginger [dʒíndʒər]
명 생강
Ginger tea is good for coughs and colds.
생강차는 기침과 감기에 좋다.

08 letter [létər]
명 편지
He gets letters from children around the world.
그는 전 세계 어린이들에게서 오는 편지들을 받는다.

09 meter [mí:tər]
명 (단위) 미터
The pool is 50 meters long.
그 수영장은 길이가 50미터이다.

10 river [rívər]
명 강
A boat is floating down the river.
보트 하나가 강을 떠내려가고 있다.

Daily Test

A 우리말 뜻과 일치하도록 빠진 글자를 써넣어 단어를 완성하세요.

1 지우개   __ r __ s __ __

2 ~ 뒤에, ~ 후에   __ __ t __ __

3 강   r __ v __ __

4 꽃   __ l __ __ __ r

5 편지   __ __ t __ __ r

B 다음 영어 단어의 우리말 뜻을 쓰세요.

1 daughter _________________

2 butter _________________

3 driver _________________

4 ginger _________________

5 meter _________________

C 우리말 뜻과 일치하도록 빈칸에 알맞은 단어를 써넣어 문장을 완성하세요.

1 A boat is floating down the _________________.
보트 하나가 강을 떠내려가고 있다.

2 The bus _________________ drives slowly around the school.
그 버스 기사는 학교 주위에서 천천히 운전한다.

3 _________________ tea is good for coughs and colds.
생강차는 기침과 감기에 좋다.

4 I closed the door _________________ they went outside.
그들이 밖으로 나간 뒤에 나는 문을 닫았다.

5 The pool is 50 _________________ long.
그 수영장은 길이가 50미터이다.

6 The _________________ is melting on the hot bread.
그 버터가 뜨거운 빵 위에서 녹고 있다.

7 She put the pink _________________ in the vase.
그녀는 그 분홍색 꽃들을 꽃병에 꽂았다.

8 Whose is the _________________ in the drawer?
서랍 안에 있는 지우개는 누구의 것이니?

11 shoulder
[ʃóuldər]
명 어깨
The man is carrying a box on his shoulder.
그 남자는 그의 어깨에 상자를 얹어 나르고 있다.

12 shower
[ʃáuər]
명 소나기
There is a strong chance of showers today.
오늘 소나기가 내릴 가능성이 크다.

13 singer
[síŋər]
명 가수
We recognized the famous singer at first sight.
우리는 그 유명한 가수를 첫눈에 알아봤다.

14 spider
[spáidər]
명 거미
Is the spider still on my head?
그 거미는 아직 내 머리 위에 있니?

15 suffer
[sʌ́fər]
동 시달리다, 고통받다   ✿ suffer from ~으로 고통받다
A lot of people suffer from depression.
많은 사람들이 우울증으로 고통받는다.

16 tiger
[táigər]
명 호랑이
It is almost impossible to see a wild tiger.
야생 호랑이를 보는 것은 거의 불가능하다.

17 tower
[táuər]
명 탑
The clock tower is worth visiting.
그 시계탑은 방문할 가치가 있다.

18 under
[ʌ́ndər]
전 ~ 아래에
What does Justin keep under the stairs?
Justin은 계단 아래에 무엇을 보관하니?

19 water
[wɔ́:tər]
명 물 동 물을 주다
The kid boiled water for his grandmother.
그 아이는 그의 할머니를 위해 물을 끓였다.

20 winner
[wínər]
명 우승자, 수상자
This year's winner will be announced soon.
올해의 수상자가 곧 발표될 것이다.

Daily Test

A 우리말 뜻과 일치하도록 빠진 글자를 써넣어 단어를 완성하세요.

1 거미   __ p __ __ e __   **2** 소나기   __ h __ __ __ r

3 호랑이   __ __ g __ r   **4** 어깨   s __ __ __ __ d __ r

5 우승자, 수상자   w __ __ n __ __

B 다음 영어 단어의 우리말 뜻을 쓰세요.

1 water   __________________   **2** suffer   __________________

3 singer   __________________   **4** tower   __________________

5 under   __________________

C 우리말 뜻과 일치하도록 빈칸에 알맞은 단어를 써넣어 문장을 완성하세요.

1 There is a strong chance of __________________ today.
오늘 소나기가 내릴 가능성이 크다.

2 The kid boiled __________________ for his grandmother.
그 아이는 그의 할머니를 위해 물을 끓였다.

3 The man is carrying a box on his __________________.
그 남자는 그의 어깨에 상자를 얹어 나르고 있다.

4 The clock __________________ is worth visiting.
그 시계탑은 방문할 가치가 있다.

5 This year's __________________ will be announced soon.
올해의 수상자가 곧 발표될 것이다.

6 We recognized the famous __________________ at first sight.
우리는 그 유명한 가수를 첫눈에 알아봤다.

7 Is the __________________ still on my head?
그 거미는 아직 내 머리 위에 있니?

8 It is almost impossible to see a wild __________________.
야생 호랑이를 보는 것은 거의 불가능하다.

Day 33 -ir-

01 bird
[bə:*rd*]
명 새
The **bird** caught worms to feed its babies.
그 새는 그것의 새끼들에게 먹이기 위해 벌레들을 잡았다.

02 birth
[bə:*r*θ]
명 탄생, 출생
Congratulations on the **birth** of your son!
너의 아들의 탄생을 축하해!

03 birthday
[bə́:*r*θdèi]
명 생일
I'm happy to be with you on my **birthday**.
나의 생일에 너희와 함께해서 행복하다.

04 chirp
[tʃə:*rp*]
동 짹짹거리다
A sparrow is **chirping** outside the window.
참새 한 마리가 창문 밖에서 짹짹거리고 있다.

05 circle
[sə́:*r*kl]
명 원형, 동그라미
Draw two **circles** on the board.
칠판에 동그라미 두 개를 그려.

06 circus
[sə́:*r*kəs]
명 서커스, 서커스단
We have ten minutes before the **circus** begins.
서커스가 시작하기 전까지 10분 남았다.

07 dirt
[də:*rt*]
명 먼지, 흙
Let's remove the **dirt** from the surface.
표면에서 먼지를 제거하자.

08 dirty
[də́:*r*ti]
형 더러운
The brothers took off their **dirty** clothes.
그 형제들은 그들의 더러운 옷을 벗었다.

09 firm
[fə:*rm*]
형 단단한, 딱딱한
You should not play soccer on the **firm** ground.
너희는 그 딱딱한 땅 위에서 축구를 하지 않는 것이 좋겠다.

10 first
[fə:*rst*]
형 첫 번째의, 제1의
Who landed on the moon for the **first** time?
누가 첫 번째로 달에 착륙했나요?

Daily Test

A 우리말 뜻과 일치하도록 빠진 글자를 써넣어 단어를 완성하세요.

1 새   __ __ __ d   **2** 먼지, 흙   __ __ r __

3 더러운   __ __ __ t __   **4** 탄생, 출생   __ i __ t __

5 서커스, 서커스단   c __ r __ __ __

B 다음 영어 단어의 우리말 뜻을 쓰세요.

1 circle   _________________   **2** firm   _________________

3 birthday   _________________   **4** first   _________________

5 chirp   _________________

C 우리말 뜻과 일치하도록 빈칸에 알맞은 단어를 써넣어 문장을 완성하세요.

1 Congratulations on the _______________ of your son!
너의 아들의 탄생을 축하해!

2 We have ten minutes before the _______________ begins.
서커스가 시작하기 전까지 10분 남았다.

3 Draw two _______________ on the board.
칠판에 동그라미 두 개를 그려.

4 A sparrow is _______________ outside the window.
참새 한 마리가 창문 밖에서 짹짹거리고 있다.

5 The brothers took off their _______________ clothes.
그 형제들은 그들의 더러운 옷을 벗었다.

6 Who landed on the moon for the _______________ time?
누가 첫 번째로 달에 착륙했나요?

7 I'm happy to be with you on my _______________.
나의 생일에 너희와 함께해서 행복하다.

8 The _______________ caught worms to feed its babies.
그 새는 그것의 새끼들에게 먹이기 위해 벌레들을 잡았다.

11 girl
[gə:rl]

명 소녀, 여자 아이
The girl shared the umbrella with her friend.
그 소녀는 그녀의 친구와 그 우산을 함께 썼다.

12 shirt
[ʃə:rt]

명 셔츠
My shirt is missing a button.
나의 셔츠에서 단추 한 개가 없어졌다.

13 sir
[sə:r]

명 (남자에 대한 경칭) 손님, 선생님
Could you sign here, sir?
여기에 사인을 해 주시겠습니까, 손님?

14 skirt
[skə:rt]

명 치마
You can choose from various styles of skirts.
너는 다양한 스타일의 치마 중에서 고를 수 있다.

15 stir
[stə:r]

동 젓다
Pour milk into the pot and stir it.
냄비 안에 우유를 붓고 저어.

16 swirl
[swə:rl]

동 빙빙 돌다, 소용돌이치다
The wind swirled around the tree.
바람이 그 나무 주위를 소용돌이쳤다.

17 third
[θə:rd]

형 세 번째의, 제3의
What is the title of the third song?
세 번째 노래의 제목은 무엇이니?

18 thirsty
[θə́:rsti]

형 목이 마른
The woman was thirsty after swimming.
그 여자는 수영을 하고 난 후에 목이 말랐다.

19 thirteen
[θə̀:rtí:n]

명 13, 열셋
She threw thirteen balls into the basket.
그녀는 바구니 안으로 공 13개를 던졌다.

20 thirty
[θə́:rti]

명 30, 서른
She bought thirty pairs of socks.
그녀는 양말 30켤레를 샀다.

Daily Test

A 우리말 뜻과 일치하도록 빠진 글자를 써넣어 단어를 완성하세요.

1 셔츠   __ h __ __ t   **2** 젓다   __ t __ __

3 30, 서른   t __ __ r __ y   **4** 치마   __ k __ r __

5 13, 열셋   __ __ __ r __ e __ n

B 다음 영어 단어의 우리말 뜻을 쓰세요.

1 sir   __________________   **2** third   __________________

3 girl   __________________   **4** thirsty   __________________

5 swirl   __________________

C 우리말 뜻과 일치하도록 빈칸에 알맞은 단어를 써넣어 문장을 완성하세요.

1 My __________________ is missing a button.
나의 셔츠에서 단추 한 개가 없어졌다.

2 What is the title of the __________________ song?
세 번째 노래의 제목은 무엇이니?

3 The __________________ shared the umbrella with her friend.
그 소녀는 그녀의 친구와 그 우산을 함께 썼다.

4 The wind __________________ around the tree.
바람이 그 나무 주위를 소용돌이쳤다.

5 Pour milk into the pot and __________________ it.
냄비 안에 우유를 붓고 저어.

6 You can choose from various styles of __________________.
너는 다양한 스타일의 치마 중에서 고를 수 있다.

7 The woman was __________________ after swimming.
그 여자는 수영을 하고 난 후에 목이 말랐다.

8 She bought __________________ pairs of socks.
그녀는 양말 30켤레를 샀다.

Day 34 -or-

01 corn
[kɔːrn]
명 옥수수
We import three hundred bags of corn every year.
우리는 매년 옥수수 300자루를 수입한다.

02 fork
[fɔːrk]
명 포크
The silver fork is too heavy to use.
그 은 포크는 너무 무거워서 사용할 수 없다.

03 horn
[hɔːrn]
명 뿔
Some animals have horns on their heads.
어떤 동물들은 머리에 뿔이 있다.

04 horse
[hɔːrs]
명 말
The black horse finished in second place.
그 검은 말은 2위를 했다.

05 pork
[pɔːrk]
명 돼지고기
They already ate three kilograms of pork.
그들은 이미 돼지고기 3킬로그램을 먹었다.

06 shorts
[ʃɔːrts]
명 반바지
Betty wears shorts when she jogs.
Betty는 조깅을 할 때 반바지를 입는다.

07 sort
[sɔːrt]
명 종류, 유형 동 분류하다
He will sort the bottles by size.
그는 그 병들을 크기에 따라 분류할 것이다.

08 sport
[spɔːrt]
명 스포츠, 운동
Skydiving is a dangerous sport.
스카이다이빙은 위험한 스포츠이다.

09 sword
[sɔːrd]
명 칼, 검
The knight pulled out his sword quietly.
그 기사는 조용히 그의 칼을 뽑았다.

10 thorn
[θɔːrn]
명 가시
A rose has a sweet smell and sharp thorns.
장미는 달콤한 향기와 뾰족한 가시들을 가지고 있다.

Daily Test

A 우리말 뜻과 일치하도록 빠진 글자를 써넣어 단어를 완성하세요.

1 포크   __ o __ __   **2** 가시   t __ __ __ n

3 말   __ __ r __ e   **4** 칼, 검   __ w __ r __

5 반바지   __ h __ __ t __

B 다음 영어 단어의 우리말 뜻을 쓰세요.

1 sort   _______________   **2** horn   _______________

3 corn   _______________   **4** sport   _______________

5 pork   _______________

C 우리말 뜻과 일치하도록 빈칸에 알맞은 단어를 써넣어 문장을 완성하세요.

1 The black _______________ finished in second place.
그 검은 말은 2위를 했다.

2 The silver _______________ is too heavy to use.
그 은 포크는 너무 무거워서 사용할 수 없다.

3 Skydiving is a dangerous _______________.
스카이다이빙은 위험한 스포츠이다.

4 We import three hundred bags of _______________ every year.
우리는 매년 옥수수 300자루를 수입한다.

5 He will _______________ the bottles by size.
그는 그 병들을 크기에 따라 분류할 것이다.

6 Betty wears _______________ when she jogs.
Betty는 조깅을 할 때 반바지를 입는다.

7 They already ate three kilograms of _______________.
그들은 이미 돼지고기 3킬로그램을 먹었다.

8 A rose has a sweet smell and sharp _______________.
장미는 달콤한 향기와 뾰족한 가시들을 가지고 있다.

11 burn [bə:rn]
- 동 불에 타다, 태우다
- They were burning leaves and branches in the yard.
- 그들은 마당에서 나뭇잎과 나뭇가지를 태우고 있었다.

12 burp [bə:rp]
- 동 트림하다
- The man drank some soda and burped loudly.
- 그 남자는 탄산음료를 마시고 크게 트림을 했다.

13 church [tʃə:rtʃ]
- 명 교회
- This building looks like a church.
- 이 건물은 교회처럼 보인다.

14 curly [kə́:rli]
- 형 곱슬곱슬한
- She tied her curly hair with a ribbon.
- 그녀는 리본으로 그녀의 곱슬곱슬한 머리를 묶었다.

15 curve [kə:rv]
- 명 곡선, 커브
- He lost control of his car on a curve.
- 그는 커브에서 그의 차의 제동력을 잃었다.

16 fur [fə:r]
- 명 털, 모피
- The rabbit has soft and white fur.
- 그 토끼는 부드럽고 하얀 털을 가지고 있다.

17 hurt [hə:rt]
- 동 다치게 하다, 아프다 ✿ hurt-hurt-hurt
- I hurt my back because of the accident.
- 나는 그 사고 때문에 나의 등을 다쳤다.

18 nurse [nə:rs]
- 명 간호사
- The male nurse led my grandpa upstairs.
- 그 남자 간호사가 나의 할아버지를 위층으로 안내했다.

19 surf [sə:rf]
- 동 파도타기를 하다
- My sister taught me how to surf.
- 나의 누나가 나에게 파도타기 하는 방법을 가르쳐 주었다.

20 turn [tə:rn]
- 동 돌다, 돌리다
- Michael turned and walked out of the room.
- Michael은 몸을 돌려서 방에서 걸어 나갔다.

A 우리말 뜻과 일치하도록 빠진 글자를 써넣어 단어를 완성하세요.

1 곡선, 커브   __ __ r __ e   2 트림하다   b __ __ __

3 불에 타다, 태우다   __ u __ n   4 곱슬곱슬한   __ u __ l __

5 털, 모피   __ __ r

B 다음 영어 단어의 우리말 뜻을 쓰세요.

1 hurt   ______________   2 church   ______________

3 turn   ______________   4 nurse   ______________

5 surf   ______________

C 우리말 뜻과 일치하도록 빈칸에 알맞은 단어를 써넣어 문장을 완성하세요.

1 This building looks like a ______________.
이 건물은 교회처럼 보인다.

2 The man drank some soda and ______________ loudly.
그 남자는 탄산음료를 마시고 크게 트림을 했다.

3 The male ______________ led my grandpa upstairs.
그 남자 간호사가 나의 할아버지를 위층으로 안내했다.

4 I ______________ my back because of the accident.
나는 그 사고 때문에 나의 등을 다쳤다.

5 They were ______________ leaves and branches in the yard.
그들은 마당에서 나뭇잎과 나뭇가지를 태우고 있었다.

6 The rabbit has soft and white ______________.
그 토끼는 부드럽고 하얀 털을 가지고 있다.

7 My sister taught me how to ______________.
나의 누나가 나에게 파도타기 하는 방법을 가르쳐 주었다.

8 She tied her ______________ hair with a ribbon.
그녀는 리본으로 그녀의 곱슬곱슬한 머리를 묶었다.

Day 35 · Review | Day 31~34

A 우리말 뜻에 해당하는 영어 단어를 찾아 동그라미 하세요.

포크	헛간, 외양간	운전자, 기사	시작하다; 시작	소녀, 여자 아이
가수	탄생, 출생	(단위) 미터	세 번째의, 제3의	파도타기를 하다

f	y	c	b	t	b	i	r	t	h
m	o	k	z	g	a	p	k	h	g
d	j	r	n	y	r	j	g	i	s
r	n	y	k	h	n	k	i	r	i
i	r	r	t	g	h	p	r	d	n
v	t	s	t	a	r	t	l	s	g
e	s	u	r	f	r	q	y	h	e
r	z	x	w	q	m	e	t	e	r

B 우리말 뜻과 일치하도록 알맞은 단어를 골라 문장을 완성하세요.

smart	arms	suffer	firm	under	horns

1 Some animals have ________________ on their heads.
어떤 동물들은 머리에 뿔이 있다.

2 What does Justin keep ________________ the stairs?
Justin은 계단 아래에 무엇을 보관하니?

3 You should not play soccer on the ________________ ground.
너희는 그 딱딱한 땅 위에서 축구를 하지 않는 것이 좋겠다.

4 The lawyer is ________________ and friendly.
그 변호사는 똑똑하고 친절하다.

5 A lot of people ________________ from depression.
많은 사람들이 우울증으로 고통받는다.

6 She lifted her ________________ straight up.
그녀는 그녀의 팔을 위로 쭉 뻗었다.

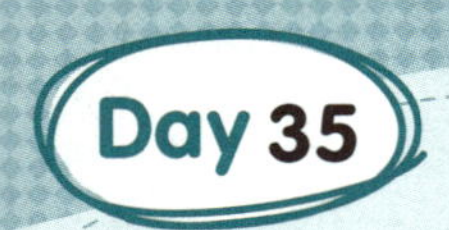

Day 35

C 들려 주는 영어 단어를 바르게 쓴 다음, 우리말 뜻을 써넣으세요.

Day 35_C

	영어 단어	우리말		영어 단어	우리말
1			11		
2			12		
3			13		
4			14		
5			15		
6			16		
7			17		
8			18		
9			19		
10			20		

D 우리말 뜻과 일치하도록 알맞은 단어를 골라 동그라미 하세요.

1 The knight pulled out his (sword / thorn) quietly.
그 기사는 조용히 그의 칼을 뽑았다.

2 He gets (erasers / letters) from children around the world.
그는 전 세계 어린이들에게서 오는 편지들을 받는다.

3 Michael (burned / turned) and walked out of the room.
Michael은 몸을 돌려서 방에서 걸어 나갔다.

4 Let's remove the (dirt / birth) from the surface.
표면에서 먼지를 제거하자.

5 Did you send the invitation (bars / cards) to your classmates?
너는 너의 반 친구들에게 초대장을 보냈니?

6 Could you sign here, (sir / first)?
여기에 사인을 해 주시겠습니까, 손님?

E 영어는 우리말로, 우리말은 영어로 바꿔 쓰세요.

1	after	___________	**2** 막대, 바	___________
3	first	___________	**4** 더러운	___________
5	tower	___________	**6** 흉터	___________
7	hurt	___________	**8** 치마	___________
9	jar	___________	**10** 지우개	___________
11	sort	___________	**12** 곱슬곱슬한	___________
13	swirl	___________	**14** 거미	___________
15	burn	___________	**16** 단단한; 열심히	___________
17	part	___________	**18** 돼지고기	___________
19	chirp	___________	**20** 강	___________

F 잘 듣고, 빈칸에 알맞은 단어를 써넣어 문장을 완성하세요.

Day 35_F

1 The kid boiled ___________ for his grandmother.

2 The black ___________ finished in second place.

3 Draw two ___________ on the board.

4 A ___________ is a musical instrument with six strings.

5 He lost control of his car on a ___________.

6 She bought ___________ pairs of socks.

7 Can you rake the fallen leaves in the ___________?

8 My ___________ likes horror movies.

Day 35

G 우리말 뜻과 일치하도록 빈칸에 알맞은 단어를 써넣어 문장을 완성하세요.

1 I'm happy to be with you on my b_______________.
나의 생일에 너희와 함께해서 행복하다.

2 The neighbor's dog sometimes b_______________ at night.
이웃의 개는 때때로 밤에 짖는다.

3 G_______________ tea is good for coughs and colds.
생강차는 기침과 감기에 좋다.

4 A rose has a sweet smell and sharp t_______________.
장미는 달콤한 향기와 뾰족한 가시들을 가지고 있다.

5 The crocodile's teeth are so s_______________.
그 악어의 이빨은 매우 날카롭다.

6 This building looks like a c_______________.
이 건물은 교회처럼 보인다.

7 This year's w_______________ will be announced soon.
올해의 수상자가 곧 발표될 것이다.

8 You should not p_______________ your car here.
너는 여기에 너의 차를 주차하지 않는 것이 좋겠다.

9 The woman was t_______________ after swimming.
그 여자는 수영을 하고 난 후에 목이 말랐다.

10 The man is carrying a box on his s_______________.
그 남자는 그의 어깨에 상자를 얹어 나르고 있다.

Review에서 틀린 문제의 영어 단어와 우리말 뜻을 쓴 다음, 영어 단어를 3번씩 쓰세요.

Answer Key

Answer Key

Day 01

p. 8

A 1 action 2 count 3 attack 4 cross
5 beat

B 1 움직임, 활동 2 배달하다 3 행동하다
4 도착하다 5 나르다

C 1 arrive 2 delivers 3 cross 4 activities
5 count 6 acts 7 carry 8 attacks

Day 01

p. 10

A 1 move 2 repair 3 walk 4 drive
5 shout

B 1 들어가다, 들어오다 2 떠나다, 출발하다
3 타다 4 따라가다, 따라오다 5 연습; 연습하다

C 1 drive 2 walking 3 enter 4 practiced
5 riding 6 following 7 shouting
8 move

Day 02

p. 12

A 1 humid 2 hard 3 light 4 loose
5 empty

B 1 거친 2 기체, 가스 3 액체; 액체의 4 얕은
5 무거운

C 1 liquid 2 loose 3 heavy 4 gas
5 light 6 shallow 7 empty 8 humid

Day 02

p. 14

A 1 wet 2 soft 3 thick 4 tight 5 solid

B 1 매끄러운, 매끈한 2 얇은, 마른
3 가파른, 비탈진 4 날카로운, 뾰족한
5 끈적거리는

C 1 tight 2 steep 3 solid 4 wet
5 sharp 6 sticky 7 thin 8 thick

Day 03

p. 16

A 1 fair 2 ancient 3 custom 4 comedy
5 different

B 1 저작권 2 고전적인; 고전, 명작 3 축제
4 전시회 5 문화

C 1 culture 2 Ancient 3 fair 4 comedy
5 different 6 exhibition 7 copyright
8 festival

Day 03

p. 18

A 1 modern 2 musical 3 tragedy
4 show 5 genre

B 1 무대 2 희곡, 연극 3 여러 가지의, 다양한
4 전통 5 비슷한

C 1 play 2 musical 3 stage 4 show
5 genre 6 tradition 7 similar
8 tragedy

Day 04

p. 20

A 1 civil 2 ban 3 allow 4 election
5 campaign

B 1 입후보자 2 민주주의 3 정부 4 선출하다
5 지배, 통제; 지배하다, 통제하다

C 1 democracy 2 civil 3 ban 4 control
5 election 6 candidates 7 government
8 campaign

A 1 policy 2 queen 3 mayor 4 law
5 obey

B 1 표, 투표; 투표하다 2 규칙, 통치; 통치하다
3 왕 4 대통령 5 정치인

C 1 law 2 queen 3 mayor 4 king
5 president 6 vote 7 politician
8 ruled

Day 05

p. 23

A

r	f	s	h	o	w	r	j	t	k
c	i	v	d	k	j	b	n	h	c
r	x	d	h	h	z	f	a	i	r
c	v	h	e	a	v	y	j	c	o
i	x	f	n	q	l	g	n	k	s
v	j	p	l	a	y	j	x	j	s
i	u	t	c	d	f	q	k	k	w
l	o	o	s	e	q	r	u	l	e

B 1 elected 2 repairs 3 classic 4 action
5 hard 6 president

C

	영어 단어	우리말
1	gas	기체, 가스
2	act	행동하다
3	copyright	저작권
4	election	선거
5	sharp	날카로운, 뾰족한
6	king	왕
7	deliver	배달하다
8	tragedy	비극
9	thin	얇은, 마른
10	ban	금지하다
11	practice	연습; 연습하다

12	festival	축제
13	light	가벼운
14	attack	공격; 공격하다
15	candidate	입후보자
16	vote	표, 투표; 투표하다
17	steep	가파른, 비탈진
18	similar	비슷한
19	ancient	고대의
20	follow	따라가다, 따라오다

D 1 rough 2 policy 3 modern 4 smooth
5 leave 6 custom

E 1 끈적거리는 2 walk 3 움직임, 활동
4 campaign 5 전통 6 comedy
7 지배, 통제; 지배하다, 통제하다 8 carry
9 습한 10 queen 11 정부 12 wet
13 시장 14 liquid 15 다른 16 genre
17 움직이다, 옮기다 18 musical
19 고체; 단단한, 고체의 20 drive

F 1 law 2 exhibition 3 empty 4 beating
5 allowed 6 enter 7 soft 8 stage

G 1 arrive 2 politician 3 culture
4 shouting 5 democracy 6 shallow
7 count 8 various 9 obey 10 tight

Day 06

p. 28

A 1 ground 2 desert 3 cave 4 beach
5 field

B 1 (바다의) 만 2 절벽 3 환경 4 숲 5 해안

C 1 field 2 desert 3 cliff 4 beach
5 cave 6 forest 7 environment
8 coast

Day 06

p. 30

A 1 sea 2 jungle 3 wave 4 rock
5 island

B 1 개울, 시내 2 언덕 3 흙, 토양 4 모래
5 산

C 1 mountain 2 jungle 3 stream 4 sea
5 hill 6 sand 7 island 8 rock

Day 07

p. 32

A 1 entire 2 confusing 3 boring
4 effective 5 amazing

B 1 재미있는, 흥미로운 2 짧은, 간단한
3 신나는, 흥미진진한
4 이용할 수 있는, 시간이 있는 5 실망스러운

C 1 disappointing 2 confusing
3 interesting 4 exciting 5 entire
6 available 7 effective 8 boring

Day 07

p. 34

A 1 possible 2 serious 3 related
4 urgent 5 worth

B 1 확신하는 2 갑자기
3 보통의, 평범한, 정상적인 4 특정한, 특별한
5 놀라운

C 1 suddenly 2 particular 3 serious
4 normal 5 related 6 sure 7 urgent
8 possible

Day 08

p. 36

A 1 earth 2 explore 3 example 4 find
5 consist

B 1 요소, 원소 2 ~이 들어 있다
3 실험; 실험하다 4 발견하다
5 조사하다, 검토하다

C 1 earth 2 contain 3 explore
4 examining 5 experiment 6 element
7 example 8 consists

Day 08

p. 38

A 1 magnet 2 space 3 planet 4 moon
5 gravity

B 1 별 2 우주, 은하계 3 실험실 4 해, 태양
5 방법

C 1 moon 2 method 3 magnets 4 star
5 planets 6 sun 7 gravity 8 lab

Day 09

p. 40

A 1 budget 2 bill 3 expense 4 borrow
5 account

B 1 (요금을) 청구하다; 요금 2 경제
3 교환하다; 교환 4 빚 5 벌다

C 1 budget 2 account 3 exchange
4 charged 5 earns 6 bill 7 borrow
8 economy

Day 09

p. 42

A 1 poor 2 lend 3 export 4 price
5 money

B 1 투자하다 2 쓰다, 소비하다 3 세금
4 수입하다; 수입 5 부유한

C 1 invested 2 import 3 price 4 spend
5 exported 6 poor 7 money 8 rich

p. 43

A

e	b	i	l	l	s	u	r	e	g
n	l	s	m	z	t	s	m	a	b
t	l	n	t	d	a	n	k	r	r
i	t	b	n	e	r	m	s	t	i
r	m	g	e	b	t	c	b	h	c
e	w	v	t	t	p	l	a	j	h
f	a	c	p	y	n	h	p	v	g
w	s	l	r	o	c	k	g	g	e

B 1 found 2 coast 3 expenses 4 brief
5 universe 6 worth

C

	영어 단어	우리말
1	cliff	절벽
2	explore	탐험하다, 탐사하다
3	disappointing	실망스러운
4	moon	달
5	hill	언덕
6	exchange	교환하다; 교환
7	particular	특정한, 특별한
8	poor	가난한
9	stream	개울, 시내
10	consist	구성되다
11	magnet	자석
12	budget	예산
13	field	들판
14	examine	조사하다, 검토하다
15	exciting	신나는, 흥미진진한
16	sun	해, 태양
17	sand	모래
18	invest	투자하다
19	serious	심각한, 진지한
20	boring	지루한

D 1 discovered 2 bay 3 lend
4 surprising 5 soil 6 earns

E 1 바다 2 possible 3 효과적인 4 beach
5 실험실 6 example 7 사막 8 economy
9 행성 10 method 11 요소, 원소
12 urgent 13 보통의, 평범한, 정상적인
14 borrow 15 수입하다; 수입 16 forest
17 밀림, 정글 18 money 19 쓰다, 소비하다
20 confusing

F 1 contain 2 charged 3 environment
4 taxes 5 related 6 amazing 7 island
8 space

G 1 account 2 mountain 3 experiment
4 exported 5 available 6 ground
7 suddenly 8 price 9 gravity
10 interesting

p. 48

A 1 check 2 effect 3 case 4 cause
5 effort

B 1 계속되다, 계속하다 2 성취하다
3 시작하다, 시작되다 4 지연, 연기; 연기하다
5 완료하다; 완벽한

C 1 begin 2 achieve 3 continued
4 delayed 5 completed 6 cause
7 effort 8 check

p. 50

A 1 result 2 goal 3 process 4 fail
5 focus

B 1 끝내다, 끝나다; 끝 2 중요한 3 성공하다
4 서두르다, 급히 가다
5 격려하다, 용기를 북돋우다

C 1 process 2 finish 3 important

4 succeed   5 encouraged   6 focuses
7 fail   8 result

Day 12

p. 52

A   1 connect   2 capital   3 global   4 citizen
5 American

B   1 언어   2 중국인, 중국어; 중국의   3 도시
4 일본인, 일본어; 일본의
5 한국인, 한국어; 한국의

C   1 city   2 capital   3 citizen   4 connected
5 American   6 Japanese   7 Korean
8 Chinese

Day 12

p. 54

A   1 London   2 world   3 Seoul   4 war
5 society

B   1 파리   2 지도자, 대표   3 거래, 무역
4 뉴욕   5 평화

C   1 society   2 leader   3 Seoul   4 Trade
5 Paris   6 war   7 London   8 New York

Day 13

p. 56

A   1 difficult   2 calm   3 correct   4 certain
5 bright

B   1 편안한   2 어두운   3 상태   4 편리한
5 바쁜

C   1 bright   2 certain   3 calm   4 difficult
5 convenient   6 condition   7 busy
8 dark

Day 13

p. 58

A   1 equal   2 thirsty   3 dirty   4 wrong

5 extreme

B   1 쉬운   2 빠른, 신속한   3 배고픈   4 준비가 된
5 필요한

C   1 wrong   2 dirty   3 necessary   4 easy
5 ready   6 extreme   7 thirsty   8 hungry

Day 14

p. 60

A   1 admit   2 image   3 forget   4 believe
5 ignore

B   1 발상, 생각   2 고려하다, 여기다   3 받아들이다
4 망설이다   5 추측하다

C   1 accept   2 ignore   3 guess   4 forget
5 admit   6 hesitate   7 considering
8 believe

Day 14

p. 62

A   1 know   2 intend   3 thought   4 judge
5 imagine

B   1 알아보다, 인정하다   2 깨닫다, 알아차리다
3 이해하다, 알아듣다   4 기억하다   5 지식

C   1 intend   2 judge   3 Imagine
4 remember   5 recognize   6 knowledge
7 know   8 understand

Day 15

p. 63

A

b	g	j	c	a	l	m	b	a	j
z	e	f	f	e	c	t	h	d	s
f	f	g	x	k	n	o	w	m	t
w	o	h	i	s	g	c	t	i	t
j	s	c	b	n	d	i	r	t	y
v	q	h	u	c	b	t	a	y	z
n	t	c	z	s	n	y	d	h	p
L	o	n	d	o	n	f	e	c	g

B 1 global 2 image 3 effort
4 knowledge 5 correct 6 case

C

	영어 단어	우리말
1	cause	원인; ~을 초래하다
2	Japanese	일본인, 일본어; 일본의
3	necessary	필요한
4	remember	기억하다
5	fail	실패하다
6	war	전쟁
7	guess	추측하다
8	condition	상태
9	American	미국인; 미국의
10	imagine	상상하다
11	bright	밝은
12	believe	믿다
13	leader	지도자, 대표
14	result	결과
15	easy	쉬운
16	judge	판단하다
17	idea	발상, 생각
18	important	중요한
19	thirsty	목이 마른
20	citizen	시민

D 1 comfortable 2 peace 3 goal
4 realized 5 language 6 quick

E 1 중국인, 중국어; 중국의 2 process
3 틀림없는, 확실한 4 world 5 성취하다
6 intend 7 무시하다 8 check
9 극도의, 극심한 10 New York
11 알아보다, 인정하다 12 dark
13 계속되다, 계속하다 14 forget
15 망설이다 16 finish 17 틀린, 잘못된
18 ready 19 사회 20 connect

F 1 Korean 2 hungry 3 delayed
4 considering 5 understand 6 Paris

7 encouraged 8 busy

G 1 capital 2 convenient 3 completed
4 equal 5 difficult 6 Hurry 7 thought
8 Seoul 9 succeed 10 accept

Day 16

p. 68

A 1 free 2 common 3 crazy 4 female
5 evil

B 1 위대한 2 성실한 3 매력적인 4 유명한
5 욕심 많은

C 1 diligent 2 famous 3 evil 4 crazy
5 female 6 greedy 7 common
8 attractive

Day 16

p. 70

A 1 polite 2 strong 3 strange 4 male
5 popular

B 1 약한, 힘이 없는 2 총명한, 똑똑한
3 참을성 있는 4 무례한 5 책임감 있는

C 1 rude 2 responsible 3 polite
4 strong 5 patient 6 weak 7 popular
8 strange

Day 17

p. 72

A 1 close 2 here 3 far 4 left 5 front

B 1 동쪽; 동쪽에 있는 2 맨 아래, 바닥
3 중심, 중앙 4 ~의 안에; 안에 5 방향

C 1 center 2 here 3 front 4 close
5 inside 6 left 7 direction 8 east

Day 17

p. 74

A 1 place 2 right 3 outside 4 near

5 west

B 1 거기에, 거기에서　2 남쪽; 남쪽에 있는
　3 북쪽; 북쪽에 있는　4 맨 위, 꼭대기; 맨 위의
　5 맞은편의; ~의 맞은편에

C 1 west　2 right　3 opposite　4 north
　5 place　6 there　7 outside　8 south

Day 18
p. 76

A 1 month　2 March　3 June　4 century
　5 January

B 1 5월　2 달력　3 2월　4 4월　5 해, 년

C 1 June　2 May　3 January　4 year
　5 March　6 century　7 February
　8 calendar

Day 18
p. 78

A 1 July　2 October　3 schedule
　4 December　5 Halloween

B 1 9월　2 추수 감사절　3 8월　4 11월
　5 크리스마스

C 1 September　2 August　3 Halloween
　4 Christmas　5 December　6 July
　7 Thanksgiving　8 November

Day 19
p. 80

A 1 advise　2 debate　3 critical　4 argue
　5 decision

B 1 ~에 반대하여　2 부인하다, 부정하다
　3 불평하다　4 결정하다　5 선택하다, 고르다

C 1 deny　2 against　3 decision
　4 advised　5 decide　6 complained
　7 choose　8 critical

Day 19
p. 82

A 1 true　2 discuss　3 oppose　4 request
　5 negative

B 1 긍정적인　2 주장하다　3 제안하다
　4 ~을 의미하다　5 추천하다, 권하다

C 1 positive　2 oppose　3 true　4 negative
　5 discuss　6 recommend　7 suggested
　8 request

Day 20
p. 83

A

c	f	h	s	d	c	r	a	z	y
e	v	n	e	w	j	t	n	J	x
n	a	M	a	r	c	h	p	u	w
t	d	d	h	m	e	g	b	l	t
e	v	t	r	u	e	r	t	y	f
r	i	l	j	t	s	o	u	t	h
j	s	z	x	b	m	v	s	d	j
w	e	a	k	w	s	d	x	c	e

B 1 bottom　2 arguing　3 free　4 April
　5 far　6 greatest

C

	영어 단어	우리말
1	north	북쪽; 북쪽에 있는
2	century	100년, 세기
3	evil	사악한
4	top	맨 위, 꼭대기; 맨 위의
5	September	9월
6	decision	결정
7	polite	예의 바른, 공손한
8	against	~에 반대하여
9	suggest	제안하다
10	close	가까운; 가까이
11	year	해, 년

12	place	장소, 곳
13	front	앞쪽; 앞쪽의
14	greedy	욕심 많은
15	Halloween	핼러윈
16	oppose	반대하다
17	critical	비판적인
18	strange	이상한
19	May	5월
20	discuss	의논하다

D 1 west 2 schedule 3 October 4 mean
5 intelligent 6 insisted

E 1 달, 월 2 diligent 3 책임감 있는
4 outside 5 부인하다, 부정하다 6 January
7 동쪽; 동쪽에 있는 8 negative
9 선택하다, 고르다 10 patient
11 8월 12 calendar 13 유명한
14 decide 15 추수 감사절 16 request
17 거기에, 거기에서 18 strong
19 가까운; 가까이 20 December

F 1 debate 2 Christmas 3 attractive
4 right 5 positive 6 February 7 male
8 inside

G 1 left 2 popular 3 November
4 recommend 5 opposite 6 female
7 complained 8 direction 9 June
10 common

Day 21

p. 88

A 1 boat 2 flight 3 highway 4 fasten
5 airplane

B 1 (교통) 요금 2 헬리콥터 3 횡단보도
4 승객 5 연료

C 1 crosswalk 2 flight 3 boat
4 helicopter 5 airplane 6 fasten
7 fare 8 passenger

Day 21

p. 90

A 1 train 2 vehicle 3 ship 4 taxi
5 truck

B 1 역, 정류장 2 바퀴 3 신호등
4 항해하다; 돛 5 지하철

C 1 taxi 2 train 3 traffic light 4 ship
5 wheel 6 station 7 truck 8 subway

Day 22

p. 92

A 1 funny 2 emotion 3 horror 4 delight
5 excited

B 1 행복 2 놀란 3 우울한 4 환상적인
5 불안해하는

C 1 depressed 2 anxious 3 horror
4 Happiness 5 delight 6 emotion
7 fantastic 8 excited

Day 22

p. 94

A 1 lonely 2 sorrow 3 worried
4 wonder 5 scared

B 1 수줍음을 많이 타는 2 초조해하는
3 자랑스러워하는 4 놀란
5 속상하게 만들다; 속상한

C 1 upset 2 shy 3 proud 4 lonely
5 worried 6 scared 7 nervous
8 wonders

Day 23

p. 96

A 1 amount 2 develop 3 factory
4 handle 5 add

B 1 증가하다, 증가시키다 2 창조하다, 만들어 내다
3 감소하다, 감소시키다 4 포함하다, 포함시키다

5 모으다, 수집하다

C 1 develop 2 add 3 factory 4 collects
5 amount 6 decreased 7 include
8 handle

Day 23

p. 98

A 1 resource 2 sell 3 produce 4 wrap
5 prepare

B 1 생산품, 상품 2 줄이다 3 다 팔린, 매진된
4 만들다 5 제공하다

C 1 reduce 2 provides 3 wrapped
4 prepare 5 sells 6 product
7 produce 8 sold out

Day 24

p. 100

A 1 map 2 corner 3 fountain 4 lead
5 downtown

B 1 시청 2 주소 3 곡선, 커브
4 주요 지형지물, 랜드마크
5 안내, 안내인; 길을 안내하다

C 1 downtown 2 leads 3 corner
4 curve 5 fountain 6 address 7 map
8 landmark

Day 24

p. 102

A 1 point 2 street 3 town 4 neighbor
5 turn

B 1 근처, 동네 2 도로 3 마을 4 옆집의
5 보여 주다, 알려 주다

C 1 village 2 pointing 3 neighbor
4 Turn 5 next-door 6 neighborhood
7 town 8 show

Day 25

p. 103

A

f	w	t	n	d	y	p	c	m	w
s	g	w	t	h	o	r	r	o	r
t	o	x	b	a	k	o	k	z	a
t	g	t	t	n	p	u	j	u	p
b	l	e	a	d	w	d	s	p	q
r	o	s	e	l	l	y	r	s	s
g	m	a	b	e	x	l	j	e	t
v	l	k	t	r	a	i	n	t	t

B 1 sailing 2 surprised 3 resources
4 collects 5 emotion 6 street

C

	영어 단어	우리말
1	fare	(교통) 요금
2	fantastic	환상적인
3	produce	생산하다
4	landmark	주요 지형지물, 랜드마크
5	ship	(큰) 배, 선박
6	shy	수줍음을 많이 타는
7	show	보여 주다, 알려 주다
8	address	주소
9	wheel	바퀴
10	factory	공장
11	reduce	줄이다
12	helicopter	헬리콥터
13	downtown	시내에, 시내로
14	nervous	초조해하는
15	neighbor	이웃 (사람)
16	traffic light	신호등
17	village	마을
18	add	추가하다, 덧붙이다
19	increase	증가하다, 증가시키다
20	delight	기쁨

D 1 created   2 next-door   3 amazed
4 station   5 guide   6 fuel

E 1 불안해하는   2 truck   3 포함하다, 포함시키다
4 lonely   5 모서리, 모퉁이   6 wonder
7 횡단보도   8 map   9 돌다, 돌리다
10 fountain   11 겁먹은, 무서워하는
12 flight   13 근처, 동네   14 prepare
15 감소하다, 감소시키다   16 taxi
17 다 팔린, 매진된   18 excited   19 승객
20 provide

F 1 amount   2 highway   3 pointing
4 funny   5 curve   6 sorrow   7 made
8 subway

G 1 develop   2 Happiness   3 city hall
4 vehicle   5 product   6 airplane
7 depressed   8 road   9 fasten
10 worried

Day 26   p. 108

A 1 balloon   2 gift   3 ceremony
4 costume   5 clock

B 1 기념일   2 오전   3 행사
4 기념하다, 축하하다   5 축하 (인사)

C 1 clock   2 ceremony   3 a.m.
4 celebrate   5 balloons   6 event
7 anniversary   8 costume

Day 26   p. 110

A 1 party   2 time   3 invite   4 watch
5 minute

B 1 ～시 (정각)   2 퍼레이드, 가두 행진
3 (시간 단위) 1시간   4 (시간 단위) 초   5 오후

C 1 party   2 minutes   3 parade
4 seconds   5 hour   6 invited   7 watch
8 p.m.

Day 27   p. 112

A 1 creative   2 ability   3 genius
4 challenge   5 expert

B 1 훌륭한, 탁월한   2 완전히 익히다, 숙달하다
3 자신감   4 (타고난) 재능이 있는
5 경쟁을 하는, 경쟁력 있는

C 1 confidence   2 expert   3 creative
4 competitive   5 genius   6 mastered
7 gifted   8 challenge

Day 27   p. 114

A 1 power   2 special   3 unusual   4 skill
5 perfect

B 1 재능   2 독창적인   3 전문적인, 전문가의
4 유일무이한, 독특한   5 힘, 장점

C 1 power   2 perfect   3 strength
4 talent   5 unique   6 professional
7 original   8 special

Day 28   p. 116

A 1 fashion   2 audience   3 article   4 film
5 advertise

B 1 방송하다; 방송   2 정보   3 오락, 오락물
4 인터뷰를 하다; 인터뷰   5 만화책

C 1 advertise   2 broadcast   3 interview
4 information   5 audience   6 articles
7 fashion   8 comic books

Day 28   p. 118

A 1 program   2 speech   3 media   4 radio
5 magazine

B 1 수행하다, 공연하다   2 기자, 리포터
3 텔레비전   4 대중의; 대중   5 신문

C 1 magazine 2 program 3 perform
4 radio 5 newspaper 6 media
7 public 8 reporter

Day 29
p. 120

A 1 hard 2 just 3 always 4 now
5 ago

B 1 이미, 벌써 2 매우, 많이 3 절대 ~ 않다
4 아래로, 아래에 5 나중에, 후에

C 1 now 2 already 3 later 4 ago
5 hard 6 always 7 never 8 much

Day 29
p. 122

A 1 soon 2 then 3 only 4 often 5 still

B 1 위로, 위에 2 보통, 대개 3 때때로, 가끔
4 잘, 좋게 5 매우, 아주, 정말

C 1 sometimes 2 Only 3 usually 4 up
5 often 6 still 7 well 8 soon

Day 30
p. 123

A

o	l	t	a	l	e	n	t	b	g
f	w	k	x	w	t	b	j	k	i
t	f	q	c	a	d	b	h	l	f
e	v	e	n	t	r	g	a	c	t
n	t	n	d	c	f	a	r	m	e
s	m	u	c	h	r	r	d	l	d
y	n	p	o	w	e	r	j	i	p
f	a	s	h	i	o	n	p	r	o

B 1 anniversary 2 ability 3 speech
4 o'clock 5 down 6 comic books

C

	영어 단어	우리말
1	ceremony	의식, 식
2	professional	전문적인, 전문가의
3	perform	수행하다, 공연하다
4	hour	(시간 단위) 1시간
5	always	항상
6	master	완전히 익히다, 숙달하다
7	second	(시간 단위) 초
8	sometimes	때때로, 가끔
9	broadcast	방송하다; 방송
10	genius	천재성, 천재
11	reporter	기자, 리포터
12	costume	의상
13	never	절대 ~ 않다
14	strength	힘, 장점
15	minute	(시간 단위) 분
16	still	아직(도), 여전히
17	article	기사
18	confidence	자신감
19	well	잘, 좋게
20	magazine	잡지

D 1 film 2 time 3 excellent 4 then
5 just 6 skills

E 1 창조적인, 창의적인 2 invite 3 오전
4 information 5 (얼마의 시간) 전에 6 only
7 보통, 대개 8 clock 9 특별한
10 original 11 청중, 관객 12 advertise
13 곧, 머지않아 14 party 15 도전
16 newspaper 17 프로그램 18 gift
19 유일무이한, 독특한 20 later

F 1 congratulations 2 perfect 3 now
4 interview 5 p.m. 6 up
7 television 8 expert

G 1 entertainment 2 balloons

3 competitive 4 very 5 media
6 celebrate 7 already 8 public
9 unusual 10 parade

Day 31
p. 130

A 1 farm 2 bark 3 card 4 harm
5 guitar

B 1 팔 2 병, 단지 3 헛간, 외양간
4 단단한; 열심히 5 막대, 바

C 1 guitar 2 farm 3 barks 4 hard
5 harm 6 bar 7 barn 8 jar

Day 31
p. 132

A 1 scar 2 start 3 part 4 star 5 smart

B 1 3월 2 마당, 뜰 3 공원; 주차하다
4 날카로운, 뾰족한 5 파티

C 1 March 2 park 3 party 4 start
5 stars 6 sharp 7 part 8 scar

Day 32
p. 134

A 1 eraser 2 after 3 river 4 flower
5 letter

B 1 딸 2 버터 3 운전자, 기사 4 생강
5 (단위) 미터

C 1 river 2 driver 3 Ginger 4 after
5 meters 6 butter 7 flowers 8 eraser

Day 32
p. 136

A 1 spider 2 shower 3 tiger 4 shoulder
5 winner

B 1 물; 물을 주다 2 시달리다, 고통받다
3 가수 4 탑 5 ~ 아래에

C 1 showers 2 water 3 shoulder
4 tower 5 winner 6 singer 7 spider
8 tiger

Day 33
p. 138

A 1 bird 2 dirt 3 dirty 4 birth 5 circus

B 1 원형, 동그라미 2 단단한, 딱딱한 3 생일
4 첫 번째의, 제1의 5 짹짹거리다

C 1 birth 2 circus 3 circles 4 chirping
5 dirty 6 first 7 birthday 8 bird

Day 33
p. 140

A 1 shirt 2 stir 3 thirty 4 skirt
5 thirteen

B 1 (남자에 대한 경칭) 손님, 선생님
2 세 번째의, 제3의 3 소녀, 여자 아이
4 목이 마른 5 빙빙 돌다, 소용돌이치다

C 1 shirt 2 third 3 girl 4 swirled
5 stir 6 skirts 7 thirsty 8 thirty

Day 34
p. 142

A 1 fork 2 thorn 3 horse 4 sword
5 shorts

B 1 종류, 유형; 분류하다 2 뿔 3 옥수수
4 스포츠, 운동 5 돼지고기

C 1 horse 2 fork 3 sport 4 corn
5 sort 6 shorts 7 pork 8 thorns

Day 34
p. 144

A 1 curve 2 burp 3 burn 4 curly 5 fur

B 1 다치게 하다, 아프다 2 교회 3 돌다, 돌리다
4 간호사 5 파도타기를 하다

C 1 church 2 burped 3 nurse 4 hurt
5 burning 6 fur 7 surf 8 curly

p. 145

Day 35

A

f	y	c	b	t	b	i	r	t	h
m	o	k	z	g	a	p	k	h	g
d	j	r	n	y	r	j	g	i	s
r	n	y	k	h	n	k	i	r	i
i	r	r	t	g	h	p	r	d	n
v	t	s	t	a	r	t	l	s	g
e	s	u	r	f	r	q	y	h	e
r	z	x	w	q	m	e	t	e	r

B 1 horns 2 under 3 firm 4 smart
5 suffer 6 arms

C

	영어 단어	우리말
1	farm	농장
2	shower	소나기
3	stir	젓다
4	March	3월
5	bird	새
6	shorts	반바지
7	star	별, 별 모양
8	thirteen	13, 열셋
9	burp	트림하다
10	flower	꽃
11	tiger	호랑이
12	harm	해, 피해; 해치다
13	sport	스포츠, 운동
14	circus	서커스, 서커스단
15	party	파티
16	fur	털, 모피
17	shirt	셔츠
18	butter	버터
19	nurse	간호사
20	corn	옥수수

D 1 sword 2 letters 3 turned 4 dirt
5 cards 6 sir

E 1 ~ 뒤에, ~ 후에 2 bar 3 첫 번째의, 제1의
4 dirty 5 탑 6 scar 7 다치게 하다, 아프다
8 skirt 9 병, 단지 10 eraser
11 종류, 유형; 분류하다 12 curly
13 빙빙 돌다, 소용돌이치다 14 spider
15 불에 타다, 태우다 16 hard 17 일부, 부분
18 pork 19 짹짹거리다 20 river

F 1 water 2 horse 3 circles 4 guitar
5 curve 6 thirty 7 yard 8 daughter

G 1 birthday 2 barks 3 Ginger 4 thorns
5 sharp 6 church 7 winner 8 park
9 thirsty 10 shoulder